LAWRENCE OF ARABIA
ZIONISM AND PALESTINE

BY SIR RONALD STORRS

SIR RONALD STORRS was one of
Lawrence's closest friends, and this
personal sketch, written in 1937
has already become a classic. Of
the chapters on Palestine which
follow, the author himself says:
"The estimate of Zionism will on
the whole be found to have stood
the test of time, and is, whatever
its demerits, at least so balanced
that each of the parties involved
continues, as in the past, to accuse
me of favouring the other." For
this edition it has been revised, and
brought up to date by a postscript
covering events down to March,
1940.

PUBLISHER'S NOTE

If you are not already on our mailing list and would
like to know when new books are added, please
send in your name and address on a postcard.
Suggestions for new additions are welcomed.

THE AUTHOR

(From a drawing by Eric Kennington in Seven Pillars of Wisdom)

Was born in Bury St. Edmunds in 1881 and educated at Charter-house and Pembroke College, Cambridge, where he obtained First Class Classical Honours. He occupied several administrative posts in the Ministry of Finance of the Egyptian Government from 1904 until 1909, when he was appointed Oriental Secretary to the British Agency in Egypt. Sir Ronald was Assistant Political Officer with the E.E.F. in 1917, Liaison Officer in Baghdad and Mesopotamia, Military, (1917–1920) and afterwards Civil Governor of Jerusalem and Judaea, Governor and C. in C. of Cyprus 1926–1932, and Northern Rhodesia 1932–1934. He knew Col. Lawrence intimately, and has given many lectures on " Lawrence of Arabia " during his recent tour in America, as well as in this country.

LAWRENCE OF ARABIA
ZIONISM AND PALESTINE

BY

SIR RONALD STORRS

PENGUIN BOOKS

HARMONDSWORTH MIDDLESEX ENGLAND

41 EAST 28th STREET, NEW YORK, U.S.A.

The Contents of this book were originally published in
"Orientations" (Ivor Nicholson and Watson) in 1937.
This selection was first published in Penguin Books in 1940.

MADE AND PRINTED IN GREAT BRITAIN FOR PENGUIN BOOKS LIMITED
BY PURNELL AND SONS, LTD., PAULTON (SOMERSET) AND LONDON

INTRODUCTION

I was pleased and proud when Mr. Allen Lane first suggested that my Lawrence chapters (IX and XVIII) in *Orientations* contained the makings of a Penguin. When, however, we came to compute we found that, assuming the quality, the quantity even after expansion (and revision) amounted to barely half a bird. I offered to build up the remainder by chapter XV, the Excursus on Zionism; and this also found favour in his eyes. The upper half, particularly when lengthened by a P.P.S. bringing it to the date of going to press, proved also much the larger; so that this particular Penguin will lurch and shuffle rather a top-heavy little fowl into the public eye.

I have tried to make each section "autarkic", but I cannot deny that Lawrence, taken out of his appropriate setting of the Hejaz episode, and Zionism, unsupported by the four long Palestine chapters which it divides, may to such as have read *Orientations* both appear relatively isolated. Yet to hatch, and to hutch these extra chapters would demand (what the Oxford English Dictionary calls) a regular "Penguinery" or "colony of pen'gwins".

The personal sketch of Lawrence would have been richer and better if I had from the first taken copies of his hundred odd letters, some ninety of which perished in the burning of Government House, Cyprus. The estimate of Zionism, which is reprinted as originally written (but brought up to 15th March, 1940, by a P.P.S.), will on the whole be found to have stood the test of time, and is, whatever its demerits, at least so balanced, that each of the parties involved continues, as in the past, to accuse me of favouring the other. I can only defend myself by accepting the double charge, and by likening my attitude (I hope with becoming reverence) to that of Hera towards Achilles and Agamemnon:

ἄμφω ὁμῶς θυμῷ φιλέουσά τε κηδομένη τε

For in her heart both of the pair
Did exercise her loving care.

The emblem on the obverse binding is my Arabic, on the reverse my Hebrew seal as Military Governor of Jerusalem (December 27, 1917, until July 1, 1920).

The unacknowledged quotations in these pages are from my diaries or private letters.

T. E. LAWRENCE

BIOGRAPHICAL SUMMARY

Thomas Edward Lawrence—always Ned to his family —was born the second of five sons at Tremadoc, in Wales, on August 16, 1888 (Napoleon's birthday), of an Anglo-Irish father and a Highland Scottish mother. He was educated at the Oxford High School for Boys, where he was already developing "a passionate absorption in the past: in heraldry, arms and armour, monumental brasses, castles, ruins, church architecture, old coins, and every fragment of brick or pottery which might throw light on the social history and ways of living of mankind".[1] He went on to Jesus College, Oxford, and gained a scholarship at Magdalen College which enabled him, under the famous archaeologist-arabist, D. G. Hogarth, to follow his bent in the Near and Middle East. In November 1914 he was appointed to the Intelligence Department of the Egyptian Expeditionary Force, Cairo. The author, seven years his senior, had preceded him there by ten years, of which he had served five in the Egyptian Government and five as Oriental Secretary to the British Agency, latterly under Lord Kitchener. By the time of Lawrence's arrival Great Britain, in retaliation for Turkish German-urged hostility, had declared Egypt (of which Turkey had been suzerain) a British Protectorate. The title of the Egyptian sovereign, Khedive, had been raised to Sultan; that of the British Representative from Agent and Consul-General to High Commissioner, his residence from

[1] *Letters of T. E. Lawrence.* Edited by David Garnett, p. 39.

Agency to Residency;[1] and this was the political status of Egypt throughout the Arabian campaigns. For Lawrence's taking over and conduct of these, the major document must always be his *Seven Pillars of Wisdom*, until his death only available to the public in the abridged *Revolt in the Desert ;* to both of which, but particularly *Seven Pillars*, the reader is referred.

After the British and Arab entry into Damascus Lawrence left the Army and served first in the Royal Tank Corps, then in the Royal Air Force, latterly as an Inspector (and perfector) of high-power motor-craft. He was retired in 1935 at the age of forty-six. On May 6, 1935, swerving his motor cycle to avoid two boys riding abreast, he was violently thrown and met his death.

[1] After the War all three were further promoted. The Sultan became King, the High Commissioner, Ambassador, and the Residency, Embassy.

LAWRENCE OF ARABIA

I

Courage! build great works—'tis urging thee—it is ever nearest the favourite of God—the fool knows little of it. Thou wouldst be joyous, wouldst thou? then be a fool. What great work was ever the result of joy, the puny one? Who have been the wise ones, the mighty ones, the conquering ones of this earth? the joyous? I believe it not.

GEORGE BORROW, *Lavengro*, chap. xviii.

Into friendship with T. E. Lawrence I know not how I entered; not at first anyhow by direct official contact. I had never heard of him until the winter of 1914, when he became a member of the Intelligence Branch of the Egypt Defence Force, and then suddenly it seemed I must have known him for many years. Lawrence was of lesser medium stature and, though slight, strongly built. His forehead was high; his face upright and, in proportion to the depth of the head, long. His yellow hair was naturally-growing pre-War hair; that is parted and brushed sideways; not worn immensely long and plastered backwards under a pall of grease. He had a straight nose, piercing gentian-blue eyes, a firm and very full mouth, a strong square chin and fine, careful, and accomplished hands. His Sam-Browne belt was as often as not buckled loose over his unbuttoned shoulder strap, or he would forget to put it on at all. Once at least I had to send my servant Ismain running with it after him into the street. Augustus John's first drawing is perfect of his Arab period; Kennington's bronze in the crypt of St. Paul's Cathedral gives the plastic and Homeric simplicity of his lines and rhythm, and Howard Coster's photograph, published in *The Illustrated London News* after his death, besides being a good likeness hints somehow at the unhappiness latent behind the eyes.

Save for official purposes he hated fixed times and seasons. I would come upon him in my flat, reading always Latin or Greek, with corresponding gaps in my shelves. But he put back in their proper places the books he did not take away; of those he took he left a list, and never failed to return them reasonably soon, in perfect condition. We had no literary differences, except that he preferred Homer to Dante and disliked my placing Theocritus before Aristophanes. He loved music, harmony rather than counterpoint, and sat back against the cushions with his eyes half-closed, enduring even that meandering stream of musical consciousness which I dignified by the name of improvisation. Ismain[1] told me that Lawrence used to ask at the door if I was alone, and go away if I was not, fearing (he told me when I complained) that he might be let in for the smart "or" the boring—he meant "and", for the terms with him were synonymous. He angered me once by failing (without excuse) to appear at a dinner of four I had arranged for him; and only told me long afterwards that I had more than "got back on him" by explaining that I shouldn't have minded if he had only warned me in time to get somebody else.

He must, it seemed, gulp down all I could shed for him of Arabic knowledge, then bounded for him by the western bank of the Suez Canal; yet never by the "pumping" of crude cross-examination. I told him things sometimes for the mere interest of his commentary. He was eager and unfatigued in bazaar-walking and mosque-hunting. I found him from the beginning an arresting and an intentionally provocative talker, liking nonsense to be treated as nonsense, and not civilly or

---

[1] My Egyptian servant, Ismail, pronounced in Egyptian Arabic, Ismain.

dully accepted or dismissed. He could flame into sudden anger at a story of pettiness, particularly official pettiness or injustice. Of all men then alive I think he trusted and confided most in D. G. Hogarth who, by making possible his Travelling Scholarship, had given him his first chance in life.

Shortly after the Arab Revolution we found that its success was being denied or blanketed by the Enemy Press (which was of course quoted by neutrals), and we decided that the best proof that it had taken place would be provided by an issue of Hejaz postage stamps, which would carry the Arab propaganda, self-paying and incontrovertible, to the four corners of the earth. The High Commissioner was quick to approve; and the Foreign Office approved him. I had corresponded with King Husain on the project, and he sent me by return of mail a design purporting to typify Islamic architecture, but to the layman indistinguishable from the Eddystone Lighthouse. This I felt would never do, so wandered with Lawrence round the Arab Museum in Cairo collecting suitable arabesque motifs in order that the design in wording, spirit and ornament, might be as far as possible representative and reminiscent of a purely Arab source of inspiration. Pictures and views were avoided, for these never formed part of Arab decoration, and are foreign to its art: so also was European lettering. It was quickly apparent that Lawrence already possessed or had immediately assimilated a complete working technique of philatelic and three-colour reproduction, so that he was able to supervise the issue from start to finish. And it seemed only a few weeks before this young Hittite archæologist was on the most intimate terms with machine-guns, with tulip bombs, even with the jealously forbidden subtleties of a Rolls-Royce engine. There still exists the last motor-cycle he had built, never ridden, never delivered, carrying ten improvements, all invented by himself.

These stamp designs (admirably carried out by the Survey Department of the Egyptian Government) drew him still more closely within the Arabian orbit and into meetings with some of my Egyptian friends, and I noticed that he grew more and more eager for first-hand knowledge. I sent my secret agent (who had assisted in the opening negotiations), to his office, to pass on all he had discovered about the Hejaz; the tribes, routes, wells, and distances. At last he asked me point blank to take him down on my next voyage to Jeddah. Nothing from any point of view could have pleased me more, and permission from his military superiors was (as he has explained) granted almost with relief. He has recorded[1] our mutual hope as we proceeded through the streets of Jeddah, that the other had not perceived that the back of his jacket was dyed bright scarlet from the leather backs of the Gun-room chairs. When Abdallah quoted Faisal's telegram saying that unless the two Turkish aeroplanes were driven off the Arabs would disperse, "Lawrence remarked that very few Turkish aeroplanes last more than four or five days. . . ."[2] Abdallah was impressed

[1] *Seven Pillars*, p. 66.

[2] His telegram to the Arab Bureau, besides admirably resuming the discussion, foreshadows unambiguously his own plan, and future position:

"17th. For Clayton:
Meeting to-day: Wilson, Storrs, Sharīf Abdallah, Azīz al-Masri, myself.
Nobody knew real situation Rābugh so much time wasted. Azīz al-Masri going Rābugh with me to-morrow.
Sharīf Abdallah apparently wanted foreign force at Rābugh as rallying point if combined attack on Medina ended badly. Azīz al-Masri hopes to prevent any decisive risk now and thinks English Brigade neither necessary nor prudent. He says only way to bring sense and continuity into operation is to have English staff at Rābugh dealing direct with Sharīf Ali and Sharīf Faisal without referring detail to Sharīf of Mecca of whom they are all respectfully afraid. Unfortunately withdrawal of aeroplanes coincided with appearance of Turkish machines but Azīz al-Masri attached little weight to them personally. He is cheerful and speaks well of Sharīf's troops."

with his extraordinary detailed knowledge of "enemy dispositions" which, being temporary Sub-Lieutenant in charge of "maps and marking of Turkish Army distribution", he was able to use with masterly effect. As Syrian, Circassian, Anatolian, Mesopotamian names came up, Lawrence at once stated exactly which unit was in each position, until Abdallah turned to me in amazement: "Is this man God, to know everything?" My journal records that "I reminded Abdallah of the permission I had that morning extracted, in his hearing from the Grand Sharīf, for Lawrence to go up to Bir Abbas; and urged him to give L. letters of introduction to Ali and Faisal". Abdallah was now so firmly gripped by Lawrence's personality that he forthwith caused his father to write this eagerly desired letter of introduction to Faisal,[1] the letter that made his dream come true; and I can still see Lawrence three days later on the shore at Rābugh waving grateful hands as we left him there to return ourselves to Egypt. Long before we met again he had already begun to write his page, brilliant as a Persian miniature, in the History of England.

[1] *Seven Pillars*, pp. 70 and 71, ". . . Storrs then came in and supported me with all his might. . . ."

II

" *A pardlike spirit beautiful and swift.*"

SHELLEY

My Baghdad journal of 15 July 1917 unsupplemented
alas, by memory, tells me: "Lawrence and Feilding
to lunch. L.'s performance in Syria little short of miracu-
lous and I hope he will get his V.C. Mentioned to me
vague Damascus possibilities."[1]

During my leave in London I heard nothing of him:
on my return to Cairo at the end of 1917 he was—
elsewhere.

Rūhi[2], whom I had instructed to watch over him in the
beginning, told me that Lawrence came to him in
Jeddah for further information about the customs and
habits of the Hejaz Arabs. Rūhi compiled for him a
vocabulary of vernacular Arabic expressions, accompanied him round the coast to Yanbo, Qaddīma, Umlej
and Wajh, and there suggested to him that he should
leave his uniform for Arab garments. At that time
(according to Rūhi), Lawrence "spoke Arabic with
horrible mispronunciation"; and though he greatly
improved his accent, he never could have passed as an
Arab with an Arab—a defect which renders his achievement the more remarkable.[3] He learnt the prostrations
of the Moslem prayer, and for a time called himself the
Sharīf Hassan, "born of a Turkish mother in Constantinople."

There are other accounts, besides those in *Seven*

---

[1] Both he and Haddād Pasha had thought of me for Military
Governor there.

[2] My Bahai Persian secret agent, mentioned on p. 12.

[3] " I could never pass as an Arab—but easily as some other native
speaking Arabic." Liddell Hart, *T. E. Lawrence*, p. 24.

Pillars, of the dynamiting of Turkish bridges[1] and culverts: none so far as I know giving the impressions of a dynamitee. This was the unsolicited introduction to Lawrence of Carl Raswan,[2] travelling on a Turkish train to Damascus:

" Somewhere near Deraa in Transjordan, as we approached a dry river bed, we were stopped, and as we looked out of the windows of our carriage, I suddenly saw and heard a terrible explosion, followed by several smaller ones. A bridge, several yards ahead of us, had been blown up with a train on it. It was ahead of our Military Convoy; our cars were shattered by falling debris, but I remember hardly anything, as we were taken away from the place of disaster and had to stay several days near Amman, until the bridge had been repaired."

Early in January 1918 I was sitting in a snowbound Jerusalem, when an orderly announced a Beduin, and Lawrence walked in and sat beside me.[3] He remained for the rest of the day, and left me temporarily the poorer by a Virgil and a Catullus. Later on, when in Jerusalem, he always stayed in my house, an amusing as well as an absorbing if sometimes disconcerting guest. He had Shelley's trick of noiselessly vanishing and reappearing. We would be sitting reading on my only sofa: I would look up, and Lawrence was not only not in the room, he was not in the house, he was not in Jerusalem. He was in the train on his way to Egypt.[4]

[1] The German General Staff pathetically records that " The destruction of 25 Railways Bridges on the Hejaz Railway line from May 1–19 shows how difficult it was to maintain the Hejaz Railway in operation."

[2] A German-American traveller-photographer of unusual artistry.

[3] *Seven Pillars*, p. 524.

[4] In England also his best friends often knew least of his whereabouts. Hogarth answered my enquiries after my Sargent drawing, lent for *Seven Pillars* in 1924: " T. E. L. (or T. E. Shaw as he now calls himself) dumps his things all over the place. It is probably either with Griggs and Co., his reproducers, or at Baker's house in Barton Street, where T. E. used to live and still I think goes

In those days and (owing to the withering hand of Monsieur Mavromatis' Ottoman concession) for years after, there was no electric light in Jerusalem, and in my bachelor household the hands of the Arab servants fell heavy upon the incandescent mantles of our paraffin lamps, from which a generous volcano of filthy smuts would nightly stream over the books, the carpets and everything in the room. Lawrence took the lamp situation daily in hand, and so long as he was there all was bright on the Aladdin front. He said he liked the house because it contained the necessities and not the tiresomenesses of life; that is to say there were a few Greek marbles, a good piano and a great many books though (I fear) not enough towel-horses, no huckabacks, and a very irregular supply of cruets and dinner-napkins. Not all my guests agreed with Lawrence's theory; but the Egyptian cook did, for my servant Saïd once observed: "When your Excellency has none other than Urenz in the house, Abd al-Wahhāb prepares *ala kaifu*—without bothering himself."

He was not (any more than Kitchener) a misogynist, though he would have retained his composure if he had been suddenly informed that he would never see a woman again. He could be charming to people like my wife and sister, whom he considered to be "doing" something, but he regarded (and sometimes treated) with embarrassing horror those who "dressed, and knew people". When at a dinner-party a lady illustrated her anecdotes with the Christian names, nick-names and pet-names of famous (and always titled) personages, Lawrence's dejection became so obvious that the lady,

---

from time to time. I can't get any replies out of T. E. He sent me some weeks ago eight chapters of his book in paged proof and I returned them with comments, but I have heard no more. Two people, Sir Geoffrey Salmond and Sir M. de Bunsen, who had been in his neighbourhood of late, reported well of T. E. to me. Alan Dawnay tells me T. E. is coming here one day in his normal fashion—without notice and refusing to be put up—but days pass and no news of him so—voilà ! "

leaning incredulously forward, asked: "I fear my conversation does not interest Colonel Lawrence very much?" Lawrence bowed from the hips—and those were the only muscles that moved: "It does not interest me at all," he answered.

I was standing with him one morning in the Continental Hotel, Cairo, waiting for Rūhi, when an elderly Englishwoman, quite incapable of understanding his talk, but anxious to be seen conversing with the Uncrowned King of Arabia, moved towards him. It was hot, and she was fanning herself with a newspaper as she introduced herself: "Just think, Colonel Lawrence, Ninety-two! Ninety-two." With a tortured smile he replied: "Many happy returns of the day."

In those days he spoke much of the press he would found in Epping Forest for the printing of the classics, where, he said: "I'll pull you the Theocritus[1] of your dreams. I'm longing to get back to my printing-press, but I have two kings to make first." He made the Kings if not the press: Faisal in Iraq, Abdallah in Transjordan stand indeed as in part his creations. But with his (and my) old friend Husain Ibn Ali of Mecca his relations were fated to fall tragically from bad to worse. That monarch was alas becoming less and less a practicable member of the Comity of Kings. Fully supported but wholly uncontrolled in his absolutism by the might of the British Empire, he dropped into the unfortunate habit of regarding the mere suggestion of anything he did not wish to do as an attack on his honour and his sovereign rights. An historian with the knowledge and the patience to go through the complete file of *al-Qibla*, for eight years the official organ of the Hāshimi Government in Mecca, could present to the world a state of mind—and of affairs—closer to the Middle Ages than to the twentieth century.

[1] To the best of my knowledge there exists no beautiful Greek text of Theocritus.

In Jeddah money for the building of a mosque was collected by the simple process of the Qaimaqam sending for persons whom the King wished to subscribe, and presenting each with a receipt prepared in Mecca for the amount to be cashed in. As late as 1923 hands were being chopped off for theft in Mecca, as prescribed by the original Shari Law. When the telegraph cable between Jeddah and Suakin broke, His Majesty hoped that the Sudan Government would withdraw their request for the customary cash deposit for its repair. Finding them obdurate, he ordered that no ship in Jeddah harbour should use her wireless under penalty of being cut off from all communication with the shore, making no exception for owners engaged on the most important business, or for time-signals. The Jeddah wireless station was kept on the watch all night in order to jam even the receipt of messages by ships, and by sending out meaningless (and sometimes obscene) signals interfered with the daily time-indication from Massawa and the correction of ships' chronometers up and down the Red Sea.

Such being the royal attitude abroad as well as at home, there was matter less for surprise than for sorrow that Lawrence's last negotiations with the man he had helped to raise so high should have been broken off in anger. Time after time the King would go back on agreements made after hours of discussion the day before. More than once he threatened to abdicate.[1] (Lawrence

---

[1] I wrote to my father during King Husain's visit to Amman in 1924, some time before his final ruin, when Sir Herbert Samuel was straining to promote an understanding between him and Ibn Sa'ud: " We are just back from Amman, where we were caught in a cloudburst, and had to remain an extra day and to return by special train through French Syria past Deraa and Sámakh to Afúleh (near Endor) with eight cars on trucks, to the wonder of the countryside. King Husain embraced me several times. We talked with him for long hours in bitter cold, and he kept turning to Clayton and me, and repeating that we were the authors of all his troubles and difficulties: which consist, as you know, in a Crown for himself, a Crown for Faisal, and a coronet for Abdallah. He gave us a banquet with seventy different kinds of dishes: the

AUTHOR WITH KING HUSAIN AT JEDDAH
December 12th, 1916

"wished he would".) I myself incline to doubt whether King Husain ever loved Lawrence. There were moments when he and his sons suspected him of working against them, and more than once let fall hints to confidants that he should not be allowed to mingle too much with the Arab tribesmen. Faisal spoke of him to me with a good-humoured tolerance which I should have resented more if I had ever imagined that kings could like king-makers.

Towards the end of my time in Jerusalem I received the notice inviting subscriptions ("by approved persons") for the original limited edition of *Seven Pillars of Wisdom*. I dispatched my cheque at once, to receive it again in a month neatly torn into four fragments, accompanied by the sharpest words I had ever known from Lawrence, to the effect that "in the circumstances" my letter was an insult, and that he was "naturally" giving me a copy, "your least share of the swag". Later he professed a cynical indifference to his magnificent gift, and, when it became known as the Twenty Thousand Dollar Book, recommended me twice to sell quickly, while the going was good. When, with his (and some joint) notes, it was burnt, he immediately collected and sent me a complete set of the original illustrations.

In the interval between Jerusalem and Cyprus I wrote to learn his plans and to suggest a meeting. He replied:

> 338171 A C Shaw,
> Hut 105
> R.A.F. Cadet College,
> Cranwell, Lincs.

1. vi. 26.

Dear R. S.,

Yes: I'm too far from London and from affairs to see many people now-a-days. Yet I hear of you and them,

---

waiters, walking up and down the tops of the tables *à la Mecque*. Lily, not happening to care about any one of the seventy, had to have a few sandwiches on our return to the house."

sometimes. If you want to see me you had better stay a week-end at Belton. We are about ten miles from it.

In August I'll be away somewhere (no notion where). Sept.-October in Cranwell, November on leave, December on a troopship for I'm on overseas draft, probably to India for a five-year spell. One of the attractions of the R.A.F. is that you see the world for nothing.

Tonsils: yes, rotten things. I haven't any. Lost them, like you.

The Sargent is reproduced and finished. The Kennington is still on the stones. The complexity and extravagance of my colour reproductions have put the Chiswick Press out of gear. They have been two years over them and are still hard at work. August, they hope to finish them. Till they do my book is held up. Yet it must come out, complete or incomplete, before I go abroad. So live in hope. Though what you will think of my personalities (yours and everybody's!) God only knows.

Au revoir,

T. E. L.

In the autumn he resumed:

2. ix. 26.

Dear Ronald,

I'll come over on Saturday the eleventh, to Belton. When? I can't yet tell you. Just carry on with what programme the overlord of Belton has: and I'll fit myself in. If Saturday is unfit for any reason (service life is highly irregular) I'll come on Sunday, and will hang about till I see you. It might be tea-time on Saturday or late, after dinner, on Sunday: but God knows. Just carry on, and I'll loom up sooner or later. I have a motor-bike, and so am mobile.

Book? November probably. Your copy will probably be posted to Colonial Office, and sent on thence by bag to the Governor and C.-in-C. of Cyprus (His Excellency; hum ha). I was exceedingly glad when I saw that news. The Sargent is at Kennington's house (Morton House, Chiswick Mall), finished with. The Kennington has been the most difficult of all the pastels,

and is not yet passed in proof. It keeps on falling to
bits: looking butcherly-like, in raw-beef blocks of red.
Very difficult. Kennington struggles hard with the colour-
printers: and I hope not vainly. All over by 15 September, for that is "binding" day, when sheets are to be
issued.

More when we meet,
Yours,
T. E. S.

My uncle forgot to warn the butler, who therefore
announced that "an airman" was at the door. Strapped
under the seat of his motor-cycle was the bound manuscript of *Seven Pillars*, one or two passages in which he
wanted me to check. When, after tea, we were pacing
up and down, round and about the lawns and gardens, I
asked him point blank why he was doing what he was
doing—and not more. He answered that there was only
one thing in the world worth being, and that was a
creative artist. He had tried to be this, and had failed.
He said: "I know I can write a good sentence, a good
paragraph, even a good chapter, but I have proved I
cannot write a good book." Not having yet seen *Seven
Pillars* I could only quote the praise of Hogarth (which
meant much to Lawrence) and agree that, compared
with the glory of *Hamlet* or *The Divine Comedy*, career
was nothing. Still, admitting these to be unattainable,
there were Prime Ministers, Archbishops, Admirals of
the Fleet, Press Barons and philanthropic millionaires,
some of whom sometimes rendered service surely pre-
ferable to this utter renunciation? He allowed the
principle, but refused the application. Since he could
not be what he would, he would be nothing: the minimum
existence, work without thought; and when he left the
Royal Air Force it would be as night-watchman in a
City warehouse.[1]

[1] This attitude is said psychologically to represent a very rare
manifestation of the *Gottmensch Komplex*.

For all his puckishness, his love of disconcerting paradox, I believed then and am certain now that Lawrence meant what he said; though I thought there was also the element of dismay at the standard expected of him by the public; and I doubted how far even his nerves could ever be the same after his hideous man-handling in Deraa.[1]

I further believe that, though not given to self-depreciation, he did underrate the superlative excellence of *Seven Pillars*, and, as a most conscious[2] artist in words, ached to go further still.

13. ix. 34.

Dear R. S.,

I have been away for a while, during which your P.C. sat on the edge of Southampton Water, peacefully, in blazing sunshine. If all of the years were like this, no man would need to go abroad. . . .

Here are your K. articles,[3] which I return because I know how rare fugitive writings become in time. Once I did three or four columns in the same paper, but I have never seen them since; they gave me the idea that newsprint is a bad medium for writing. The same stuff that would pass muster between covers looks bloodless between ruled lines on a huge page. Journalistic writing is all blood and bones, not for cheapness' sake, but because unnatural emphasis is called for. It's like architectural sculpture which has to be louder than indoor works of art.

So I'd say that these articles of yours read too "chosen" for press-work; but that in a book they would be charming. You write with an air . . . and airs need the confinement of walls or end papers or whatnots

[1] *Seven Pillars*, chap. xxxv. More than one member of his Staff told me that, after Deraa, they felt that something had happened to Lawrence which had changed him.
[2] Too conspicuous sometimes, as for instance in the effort to avoid ending *Seven Pillars* with the weak but natural phrase " how sorry I was ".
[3] On Lord Kitchener from *The Times*.

to flourish. But do airs flourish ? I think they intensify, suffuse, intoxicate. Anyhow they are one of the best modes of writing, and I hope you will try to write, not fugitive pieces, but something sustained or connected by the thread of your life.

. . . . .

I've often said to you that the best bit of your writing I ever read was your dictated account of the report of an agent's interview, pre-revolt, with the Sharif of Mecca on his palace roof at night. If you could catch atmosphere and personality, bluntly, like that, it would be a very good book. These K. articles might be blunted. You'll have to use the word "I" instead of the bland "Secretary" . . .[1] Forget the despatch and the F.O. and try for the indiscreet Pro-consul !

Yours,

T. E. S.

He loved discussing his own prose and, if convinced, was humble under criticism, whether of style or of fact. When I told him that he had been too generous to me in the beginning of his book but not quite just in the middle,[2] where, if I was "parading", it was in order to teach him a business at which he was new and I was old, he exclaimed that he would have altered the passage had he known in time.

My wife and I came upon him early in 1929 returning from India by the *Rajputana*, where he spent his time, flat in his berth, translating Homer. He did not dissent when I thought that his *Odyssey* sacrificed overmuch to the desire of differing from predecessors: for instance in rendering ροδοδάκτυλος ἠώς—rosy fingered dawn —in nineteen different ways. It is therefore an arresting rather than a satisfying version. Lawrence, though respectful almost to deference of expert living authority,

---

[1] Necessary because the articles were anonymous and therefore in the third person.
[2] *Seven Pillars*, p. 98.

lacked the surrender of soul to submit himself lowly and reverently, even to the first poet. Of Matthew Arnold's three requisites for translating Homer—simplicity, speed and nobility, all dominating qualities of Lawrence's being—he failed somehow in presenting the third, substituting as often as not some defiant and most un-Homeric puckishness of his own, so that Dr. Johnson's criticism of Pope's *Iliad* would be no less applicable to Lawrence's Revised Version. The classical Arab could become in a trice a street Arab. Nevertheless, Lawrence's *Odyssey* possesses two outstanding merits. It represents Lawrence as well as Homer, and it has by hero-worship or the silken thread of snobbishness led to Homer thousands that could never have faced the original, or even the renderings of Pope, Chapman, or Butcher and Lang; just as for countless Londoners the "approach" to the Portland Vase, visible but neglected for a century in the British Museum, was induced through its auctioning at Christie's in the presence of the Prince of Wales.

Lawrence sent me in Cyprus, inviting comment, the typescript of *The Mint*, a remarkable and sometimes brutal picture of his early days in the Air Force. The narration was no less fine than the description, but the contrast between the lives and the language of all ranks was startling indeed. It seemed that they could only find relief from the cloistered rigour of their existence by expressing their emotions with an almost epileptic obscenity.[1] I offered, by a necessary minimum of blue pencil over a total of some thirty pages, to enable the book to emerge from the steel safe in which I had to guard it when not in use, into general reading: but Lawrence said the language was the life, sooner than falsify which he would rather not publish at all. (Part

---

[1] Perhaps on the precept of Catullus:
  " Nam castum esse decet pium poetam
  Ipsum, versiculis nihil necesse est."

having appeared during his lifetime in an English news-paper, under a misapprehension that he had approved thereof, a copyrighting publication of 10 copies prohibi-tively priced was arranged in America; none other to appear until his earliest authorized date of 1950.)

He hated public attention save when impersonal enough for him to appear not to notice it, but was not disappointed when, as nearly always, his incognito broke down. One day he offered to take my wife and me to the Imperial War Museum "to see the Orpens". When we came to his portrait by James McBey, I asked him to stand in front so that we might for a minute see him against McBey's vision. In a flash the word went round the Staff that Lawrence was here, and for the rest of our visit we were accompanied by the rhythmic beat of a dozen martial heels. Lawrence was clearly not displeased, yet when on our departure I remarked upon the number of our escort, "Really?" he said "I didn't notice any one." He was indeed a mass of contradictions: shy and retiring, yet he positively enjoyed sitting for, and criticizing, his portrait. No one could have been more remote from the standard of the public school, and I can as easily picture him in a frock-coat or in hunting pink as in an old school tie. In action likewise he was an individual force of driving intelligence, but with nothing of the administrator; having about as much of the team spirit as Alexander the Great or Mr. Lloyd George.

In England we met (as might have been expected) more often unexpectedly than by appointment—in the street, on a bus, or at a railway station. Once, when I was choosing gramophone records, a hand from behind descended firmly upon my shoulder. I had only just arrived in England, and supposed for a moment that this must be an attempt on the part of an assistant at Brighter British Salesmanship. It was Lawrence, replenishing the immense collection of records arranged in volumes round a square of deep shelves in the upper room of his cottage. On another occasion he led me to his publishers where, walking round the room, he picked out half a dozen expensive books, and, as though he were the head of the firm, made me a present of them.[1] He was a loyal, unchanging and affectionate friend, and would charge down from London on the iron steed from which he met his death to visit me in a nursing home, or run up 200 miles from the West of England to say good-bye before I returned to Cyprus. After a convalesence voyage he wrote

> 338171 A/c Shaw,
> R.A.F. Cattewater,
> Plymouth.
> 5. v. 29.

Dear R. S.,

Maurice Baring told me you were back. Did it do good? Are you fit, or fitter even?

I'm down here, too far off to reach London even for a week-end: but the place is good, and the company. So all's well with me.

Please give my regards to Lady Storrs. I hope she is contented with your improvement.

M. B. has given me a huge *Gepäck*[2] five times as fat as yours, and stuffed full of glory. I did not know there were so many good poems, in it, and outside it. Half of it is strange to me.

> Yours,
> T. E. S.

Leaving Southampton for Canada in 1934 we were " greeted[3] by C.P.R. officials and by T. E. Shaw. Him I found, healthier in appearance than ever before, capless in brown overalls and blue jersey. He came

[1] They included that deservedly successful War book *The Enormous Room* which the firm had only published on his strong recommendation.

[2] Maurice Baring made some twelve *Gepäcks*: small square volumes of blank pages on which were pasted poems and extracts from poems cut from other books and forming polyglot anthologies.

[3] Canadian Diary.

aboard and talked awhile of his retirement next March to a small cottage on a maximum of £100 per annum. He would provide bread, honey, and cheese for visitors, but could not put them up otherwise than in a sleeping-bag (marked Tuum—his own Meum) on the floor. In order to side-slip the photographers he took me in his Power-boat *Joker* (£180, 25 knots, unupsetable) and allowed me to zigzag it about for 15 minutes. A permanent friend I shall always rejoice to see, with generosities of feeling for persons as well as for books." I never saw him again alive.

Nine-tenths of his letters to me have perished, and only a half-dozen, which never left England, remain. Even these few reveal his power and variety in that rarely mastered art. I had in a moment of weakness consented to ask him to write an introduction to a book on Beduin Life by an artist whose exhibition I had opened. I knew the request was hopeless, and had only written *par acquit de conscience* begging him at least to let me have an answer I could pass on. His reply, though admirable and richly deserved, hardly fell within this category.

Bridlington,
25. ii. 35.

No: I won't; Forewords are septic things, and I hope never to do another. Bertram Thomas was like the importunate woman; but to strangers it is easy to say "No": he must understand that he has no claim on me: nor do I even know what he has written, or why, or who he is. No, most certainly No.

Yours,
T. E. S.

I leave here to-morrow a.m. . . . and the R.A.F. that same moment εἶθε δὲ μήδ' . . . [1]

---

[1] From the Greek epitaph of despair

ενθάδε κείμαι

Ταρσεύς · μὴ γήμας · εἶθέ δὲ μήδ' ὁ πάτηρ.

" Here lie I of Tarsus
Never having married, and I would that my father had not."
Mackail, *Select Epigrams*, p. 172, 1911.

Bridlington
25. 2. 35

NO : I won't ; Forewords are
septic things , and I hope never to do
another Bertram Thomas was like the
unfortunate woman ; but to strangers it is
easy to say " NO": he must understand
that he has no claim on me : nor do I even know
what he has written , or why, or whether. No,
most certainly No .

Yours
TES

I leave here tomorrow a. m. ... and the R.A.F.
that same moment εἰθὶ δὲ μήδ

Lawrence hated Society, but loved company. He refused the post of Director of Archaeology in Cyprus because of what he chose to imagine the social obligations of an official there. Those who knew him could have predicted the comparative failure of his Fellowship of All Souls, where it is reasonably expected of members to mingle with their fellows and—if not indeed to roll the ghost of an Olympian (a Cambridge accomplishment)—at least to present to the Common Room on occasion a polished spook of Horace. "Conversation", says Gibbon, of the most famous Arab, "enriches and enlivens the mind, but solitude is the school of genius."

Nevertheless, Lawrence liked sometimes to walk and talk with friends. The simplicity of his life was extreme. He smoked no tobacco, he drank no alcohol; but alas, he used a drug. His drug was speed, and speed was the dope which cost him his life. He once raced along the open road against an aeroplane, and led it for nearly a quarter of an hour.

Consider the variety of elements in his composition. It has been given to few to achieve greatness and also to enshrine that greatness in splendid prose: to which other of these few has been added the fastidious artistry to plan every detail of the setting up, the illustration, the printing and the binding of the material presentation of his genius ? On any topic he was one of those who let fall, whether in speech or writing, the creative and illuminating idea or phrase—unmistakably his, signed all over—which held your memory and recharged your intellectual and spiritual batteries.

Lawrence suffered acutely from public exaggeration in all directions. Like Bassanio he had chosen the leaden casket—"Who chooseth me must give and hazard all he hath." And his reputation when alive, and even after, has been subjected by some to a steady dribble of depreciation. There was a lack of understanding from moral as well as intellectual inferiors, who had occupied higher offices than his but had perhaps distinguished themselves less therein. And it was from such that he knew the bitterness, the contemptuous bitterness of irrefutable calumny. We are told that his military operations were on a small scale. So were those of Thermopylae and of Agincourt. We are told that anybody could have done what he did, with Allenby behind him, backed by the golden sovereigns of the British Treasury. But Paladins of the stamp and stature of an Allenby do not accord themselves, nor the resources of the British Treasury to an "anybody". He was actually accused of a publicity engineered by intentional mystification; and indeed it must have irritated some other public servants to find a man without a handle before his name or letters after it, without a dress suit and with an income of under a hundred a year, nevertheless pursued and chronicled by an eager limelight which seemed in comparison to black out their particular merits. I have even heard his strong columns of English belittled as having been built, as he said himself, upon the foundation of Doughty; and true it is, that Doughty was no less his literary ancestor, than Gibbon Macaulay's. Dante gloried in "taking his fine style from his master", Virgil. If Lawrence lit his candle from Doughty's flame, was the candle any less his own? There are two classes of public servant. Of one it is said: "What is he doing now?" Of the other: "Who is Minister of this or Governor of that." The first category will interest and arrest and fascinate the world. Lawrence was one of those first. Mr. Winston Churchill is one of them, and so is Mr. Lloyd George. The second, a far more numerous category—will be identified as occupying most of the best places.

Lawrence was throughout the last months of his life oppressed by gloomy forebodings. In one of his later letters he spoke of "an utterly blank wall" after leaving his beloved R.A.F.; one of his latest to me[1] ends with the three hopeless words of the man of Tarsus.

> Ozone Hotel,
> Bridlington,
> Yorks.
> 31. i. 35.

Dear R. S.,

No; alas, Hythe will know me no more. I have only a month to do in the R.A.F. and will spend it up here, overseeing the refit of ten R.A.F. boats in a local garage. The name of the Hotel is real. So, I think, is the ozone, or is it the fishmarket that smells. It is empty, cold, and rather nice.

. . . . .

Alas, I have nothing to say at the moment. After my discharge I have somehow to pick up a new life and occupy myself—but beforehand it looks and feels like an utterly blank wall. Old age coming, I suppose; at any rate I can admit to being quite a bit afraid for myself, which is a new feeling. Up till now I've never come to the end of anything.

Ah well. We shall see after the Kalends of March. Indeed, I venture to hope we shall see each other, but I don't know where I shall live, or what do, or how call myself.

. . . . .

Please regard me to Lady Storrs: and please make yourself again into fighting trim: or perhaps you are, now. Good.

> Yours,
>
> T. E. S.

Here is the second half of what was probably his very last letter, written on Jubilee Day to Eric Kennington:

You wonder what I am doing? Well, so do I, in truth. Days seem to dawn, suns to shine, evenings to

[1] P. 27.

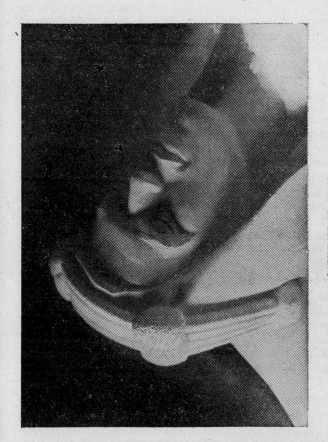

LAWRENCE OF ARABIA

(By Eric Kennington In The Kennington Memorial at Dorchester Church)

B

follow, and then to sleep. What I have done, what I am doing, what I am going to do puzzle and bewilder me. Have you ever seen a leaf fallen from your tree in autumn and been really puzzled about it ? That's the feeling. The cottage is all right for me . . . but how on earth I'll be able to put any one up baffles me. There cannot ever be a bed, a cooking vessel, or a drain in it— and I ask you . . . Are not such things essential to life . . . necessities ? Peace to everybody.

Lawrence items carried a news value of hard cash, so that when at the end of his Air service he returned to the cottage at Clouds Hill, his welcome home was a row of strange faces blinking and dodging behind a battery of cameras. He fled the place awhile, then crept in, he hoped secretly, by night. They stoned his roof to make him appear. One forced his way in. Lawrence went for him, knocked him down and threw him out. His friend found him trembling—"so many years since I've struck a man". There is no close season for heroes.

Every day, for the last three weeks of his life, a bird would flutter to his window, tapping incessantly with its beak upon the pane. If he moved to another window, the bird followed and tapped again. The strange insistence was so visibly fraying his nerves that one morning, when he had gone out, his friend shot the bird.[1] In that same hour, wrenching his handle-bars for the last time, Lawrence was flung over them sixty feet head first on to the granite-hard tarmac.

I stood beside him lying swathed in fleecy wool; stayed until the plain oak coffin was screwed down.

[1] Virgilians will be reminded of the *Diva* which Jupiter sent in the shape of a little bird to dash herself against the shield of Turnus in his last fight with Aeneas (*Aeneid* XII, 861 . . .):

" Alitis in parvae subitam collecta figuram,
quae quondam in bustis aut culminibus desertis
nocte sedens serum canit importuna per umbras—
hanc versa in faciem Turni se pestis ob ora

There was nothing else in the mortuary chamber but a little altar behind his head with some lilies of the valley and red roses. I had come prepared to be greatly shocked by what I saw, but his injuries had been at the back of his head, and beyond some scarring and discoloration over the left eye, his countenance was not marred. His nose was sharper and delicately curved, and his chin less square. Seen thus, his face was the face of Dante with perhaps the more relentless mouth of Savonarola; incredibly calm, with the faintest flicker of disdain. The rhythmic planes of his features gradually became the symbolized impression of all mankind, moulded by an inexorable destiny. Nothing of his hair, nor of his hands was showing; only a powerful cowled mask, dark-stained ivory alive against the dead-white chemical sterility of the wrappings. It was somehow unreal to be watching beside him in these cerements, so strangely resembling the *aba*, the *kuffiya* and the *aqàl* of an Arab Chief, as he lay in his last littlest room very grave and strong and noble. Selfish, to be alone with this splendour; I was sorry, too late, that neither

---

fertque refertque sonans clipeumque everberat alis.
illi membra novus solvit formidine torpor. . . ."

E'en thus the deadly child of night
Shot from the sky with earthward flight.
Soon as the armies and the town
    Descending, she descries,
She dwarfs her huge proportion down
    To bird of puny size,
Which perched on tombs or desert towers
Hoots long and lone through darkling hours:
In such disguise the monster wheeled
Round Turnus' head and 'gainst his shield
    Unceasing flapped her wings:
Strange chilly dread his limbs unstrung:
Upstands his hair: his voiceless tongue
    To his parched palate clings.
        (Conington's translation.)

Turnus was of the clan *Laurens*:
  "non fuit excepto Laurentis corpore Turni."
        (*Aen.* VII, 650.)

Augustus John nor Eric Kennington, though both within a few hundred yards, should have had the chance to preserve it for the world. As I looked I remembered that my first sight of death had been my beloved Arabic tutor at Cambridge, thirty-one years before, Hassan Tewfik ibn Abd al-Rahman Bey al-Adli—may God be well pleased with them both. Suddenly, in a flash, as by a bolt from the cloudless serene he had been wrapt into eternity, and we may well believe that his adventurous spirit leapt gladly to the call, as the trumpets sounded for him on the other side. As we carried the coffin into and out of the little church the clicking Kodaks and the whirring reels extracted from the dead body their last "personal" publicity.[1]

Some knew one side of Lawrence, some another. I wondered then if any knew him at all, or could imagine what had been his purpose, what the frontiers of his being. Could he have grown old? Had he ever been young? Some think he intended to resume action, for his country. Others that he would have created at least one more great work, for like Plato he felt deeply that what gives life its value is the sight, however revealed, of Eternal Beauty. In this he is with the great Elizabethans—Sir Philip Sidney; with the great Victorians —Charles Gordon—whose whole lives, free from fear and gain (those old perverters of mankind) are a protest against the guaranteed, the pensioned, the standardized and the safety-first existence. Like them Lawrence, even without his work, without his book, was and remains a standard and a touchstone of reality in life.

[1] Immediately after his death a perverse cult was started, mainly by owners of the privately printed *Seven Pillars* and other monopolists in *Lawrenciana*, of horror at the desecration whereby that masterpiece was made available for the outside world; bringing back to me the protests of the Wagnerian fervent, when others beside the Bayreuth pilgrims were at last privileged to enjoy *Parsifal*.

That vast convulsion of human nature, the Great Four Years' War, may have thrown up more important world-figures; none more gallantly yet practically romantic than the shy, slight, unaccountable emanation of genius who will live in universal as well as in English history as Lawrence of Arabia.

PART II

ZIONISM AND PALESTINE

Vere scire est per causas scire

I

I must warn those not interested in this question to beware. Though the territory involved is in extent negligible, though the inhabitants have produced nothing that has mattered to humanity, nevertheless, the problem of reconciling their rights and grievances with the promises made to and the aspirations cherished by an Israel that has meant and still means so much to the world, is apt to become an obsession, rarely accompanied by temperance, soberness or justice. So I summon up my heart to write dispassionately of Zionism under the three Military and the first two Civil Administrations, adding perhaps later comment; well aware that I may be risking thereby the toleration of my Jewish, the confidence of my Arab, the respect of my Christian friends.

Zionism is viewed from four different aspects. By enthusiastic supporters, minimizing difficulties and impatient of delay: these comprise I suppose a fair proportion of universal Jewry and many Gentiles outside Palestine. By declared adversaries, including all Palestinians who are not Jews, Roman Catholics (uninterested in the Old Testament) all over the world, and British sympathizers with Moslem or Arab views not concerned with formulation or maintenance of world policy. By persons unconcerned, or suspending or unable to form a judgment (I suppose about one thousand millions). By the official on the spot, loyal to the Mandate his country has accepted, yet wishing to justify his office to his conscience; and by persons connected with the British Government and Legislature, the League of Nations and

41

the Press. I respectfully address myself to all four categories.

What does the average English boy know of Jews? As Jews, nothing. At my first school, between the age of seven and ten, I had met a Ladenburg, and a charmingly mannered Rothschild who seemed to know everything, in the sense that you could tell him nothing new, and who impressed me (as have other Jews later in life) with a sense of unattainable mental correctness. He did not come to school on Saturday (which I envied), and was not allowed to be flogged (which I resented). At Charterhouse were two pleasant brothers Oppé (very much cleverer than myself), who appeared in chapel at half-past seven every morning with the rest of us. At Cambridge Ralph Straus was one of my best friends but I do not think it ever occurred to either of us, that he was a Jew. There must have been other Jews in these institutions, but neither I nor my companions knew them as Jews. I never heard my father mention Jews save in connection with the Old Testament, outside of which apart from an occasional Rabbi he had hardly met one. My mother used to recall with relish how she had let our house at Westgate-on-Sea to a well-known Jewish family; excellent tenants, but so orthodox that they had taken down and inadvertently left in the cellar all our "sacred" pictures—including a reproduction of Van Dyck's Infant Son of Charles the First. In Egypt I soon met and still enjoy the friendship of the leading Jews, a powerful colony of Sephardim originally from Italy, Damascus and Salonika. I was invited to the weddings and other festivals of the Suares, Rolo, Cattaui, Menasce, Mosseri and Harari; their Rabbis occasionally consulted me as Oriental Secretary—so much so that my appointment to Jerusalem was, according to Rabbi della Pergola, fêted in the Synagogue of Alexandria. Like their predecessor Joseph and like Sir Solomon de Medina, knighted by

King William III at Hampton Court in 1700, they were loyal to the country of their adoption, and as bankers and Government officials enjoyed and deserved good reputations. As with all Jews, there was usually a crisis of some sort or other in the internal organization of their Kehilla—Jewish Community—of which you could hear widely differing versions in the bazaars and in the aristocratic Kasr al-Dubara. Their leaders were consulted with advantage, alike by Khedivial Princes and by British Representatives.

This then, apart from the Old Testament (Psalms almost by heart) and Renan's *Histoire du Peuple d'Israel*,[1] was the sum of my knowledge of Jewry until the year 1917, a limitation which Providence was pleased to mitigate for me in middle life. My wife had never met a Jew until she reached Jerusalem after our marriage in 1923. I had much and still have much to learn. Nevertheless, having loved Arabic throughout my career—with the Egyptians, who speak it best, and the Palestinians, whose citadel of identity it is; having played a small part in the Arab National Movement; having studied and admired Jewry, having received much kindness from many Jews (and been pogromed in their Press as have few other Goys[2] or with less cause); above all, having been for the first nine years of the British Administration Governor of Jerusalem, striving according to my lights for the good of all creeds, I should feel it cowardly to omit my experiences of the early and the later working of Zionism. Being neither Jew (British or foreign) nor Arab, but English, I am not wholly for either, but for both. Two hours of Arab grievances drive me into the Synagogue, while after an

[1] I read him again in Jerusalem: "a little out of date, but very stimulating: not very popular with the Jews, who dislike (for instance) Abimelech being described (rightly) as a worshipper of Moloch. Renan himself venerates the Patriarchs and the Prophets, but appears to dislike all between them".

[2] Gentile or non-Jew.

intensive course of Zionist propaganda I am prepared to embrace Islam.

Europe had learned before, during and particularly after the War, the full significance of Irredentism (invented but unfortunately not copyrighted by Italy): practical Zionism, or Irredentism to the nth, was new to most and stood alone. I happened to have learned something of it from the chance of my few weeks in the War Cabinet Secretariat; but with 95 per cent. of my friends in Egypt and Palestine (as in England) the Balfour Declaration, though announcing the only Victory gained by a single people on the World Front, passed without notice; whilst the few who marked it imagined that the extent and method of its application would be laid down when the ultimate fate of Palestine (assuming the conquest of its northern half and final Allied victory) had been decided. Those who had heard of the Sykes-Picot negotiations in 1916 cherished vague hopes of Great Britain being awarded Haifa as a British Possession. Mandates were unknown, though President Wilson's Fourteen Points seemed to indicate that Palestinians (then generally considered as Southern Syrians) would be allowed some voice in their political destiny. By the early spring of 1918 O.E.T.A.[1] was already beset with, and its seniors working overtime upon, new and strange problems.

When therefore early in March Brigadier General Clayton showed me the telegram informing us of the impending arrival of a Zionist Commission, composed of eminent Jews, to act as liaison between the Jews and the Military Administration, and to "control" the Jewish population, we could hardly believe our eyes, and even wondered whether it might not be possible for the mission to be postponed until the status of the Administration should be more clearly defined. How-

[1] Occupied Enemy Territory Administration (South): known and pronounced in three syllables as O.E.T.A.—O-EETA.

DR. CHAIM WEIZMANN
Bronze by Jacob Epstein)

ever, orders were orders; and O.E.T.A. prepared to
receive the visitors. Confidential enquiries revealed
Arab incredulity of any practical threat. Zionism had
frequently been discussed in Syria. Long before the
War it had been violently repudiated by the Arab
journal *al-Carmel* as well as officially rejected by the
Sultan Abd al-Hamīd in deference to strong Moslem
feeling;[1] to which it was presumed that a Christian
Conqueror who was also the greatest Moslem Power
would prove equally sensitive. The religious Jews of
Jerusalem and Hebron and the Sephardim were strongly
opposed to political Zionism, holding that God would
bring Israel back to Zion in His own good time, and that
it was impious to anticipate His decree.

The Zionist Commission travelled by train from
Egypt, and after some *contretemps* whereby they were
marooned awhile on the platform of Lydda Station,
arrived by car in Jerusalem. I received in the Governorate Major Ormsby-Gore,[2] and Major James de Rothschild, Political Officers, Lieut. Edwin Samuel, attached,
Mr. Israel Sieff, Mr. Leon Simon, Dr. Eder, Mr. Joseph
Cowen and Dr. Chaim[3] Weizmann, President of the
World Zionist Organization. Monsieur Sylvain Lévy,
an anti-Zionist, was attached to the Commission as
representative of the French Government. The party
being under the official aegis of the British Government,
I assembled in my office the Mayor of Jerusalem and
the Heads of Communities in order that they and the
visitors should meet, for the first time anyhow, in
surroundings at once official and friendly. The Jerusalem
faces were unassuring. I find among my letters home

[1] In 1911 Messrs. Nossig, Frumkin and Knesevitch had been
discouraged by the British Agency in Cairo from buying land
between Rafa and Arish. The intended introduction of Jews
was noticed unfavourably in the Egyptian Press.
[2] Afterwards Secretary of State of the Colonies. Succeeded his
father as Lord Harlech.
[3] Russian spelling: pronounced in English *Háyyim*.

the plan of the dinner party with which I followed up this first meeting, annotated for my mother's information:

| Mr. Abu Suan of Latin Patriarchate | Mūsa Kāzem Pasha al Husseini, Mayor of Jerusalem | Mr. Silvain Lévy,[1] French Orientalist | The Mufti of Jerusalem[2] | Sa Grandeur Thorgom Kushagian, Armenian Bishop of Cairo (acting Armenian Patriarch) | Arif Pasha Daudı, ex-Ottoman Official of good family |

Major Ormsby-Gore

| Mr. D. Salāmeh, Vice-Mayor of Jerusalem (Christian Orthodox) | Major J. de Rothschild | His Eminence Porphyrios, Archbishop of Mount Sinai, Locum Tenens Orthodox Patriarchate | Military Governor | Lt.-Col. Lord Wm. Percy Dr. Weizmann | Ismail Bey al Husseini, Director of Education |

After proposing "The King" I explained that I had seized the occasion of so many representatives of communities being gathered in Jerusalem to clear away certain misunderstandings aroused by the visit of the Zionist Commission. Dr. Weizmann then pronounced an eloquent exposition of the Zionist creed: Jews had never renounced their rights to Palestine; they were brother Semites, not so much "coming" as "returning" to the country; there was room for both to work side by side; let his hearers beware of treacherous insinuations that Zionists were seeking political power—rather let both progress together until they were ready for a joint autonomy. Zionists were following with the deepest sympathy the struggles of Arabs and Armenians for that freedom which all three could mutually assist each other to regain. He concluded: "The hand of God now lies heavy upon the peoples of Europe: let us unite in prayer that it may lighten." To my Arabic rendering of this speech the Mufti replied civilly,

[1] Who withdrew from the Commission and Organization during the Peace Conference.

[2] Kāmel Effendi, who died 1922, and is not to be confused with his successor, Haj Amin Effendi, the present ex-Mufti of Jerusalem.

thanking Dr. Weizmann for allaying apprehensions which, but for his exposition, might have been aroused. He prayed for unity of aim, which alone could bring prosperity to Palestine, and he quoted, generalizing, a *Hadith*, a tradition of the Prophet, "Our rights are your rights and your duties our duties".

It had been from a sense of previousness, of inopportunity, that Clayton and I had regretted the immediate arrival of the Zionist Commission; certainly not from anti-Zionism, still less from anti-Semitism. We believed (and I still believe) that there was in the world no aspiration more nobly idealistic than the return of the Jews to the Land immortalized by the spirit of Israel. Which nation had not wrought them infinite harm ? Which had not profited by their genius? Which of all was more steeped in the Book of Books or had pondered more deeply upon the prophecies thereof than England ? The Return stood indeed for something more than a tradition, an ideal or a hope. It was The Hope— Miqveh *Yisroel*, the Gathering of Israel, which had never deserted the Jews in their darkest hour—when indeed the Shechinah had shone all the brighter,

"a jewel hung in ghastly night".

In the triumph of the Peace the wrongs of all the world would be righted; why not also the ancient of wrongs ?

Zionism was created by the Diaspora; throughout the ages it has slept but never died. A remnant shall return[1], shall return with joy; "next year in Jerusalem". In Russia, where Jewish suffering if not bitterest certainly lasted longest, there appeared in the last century the *Hovevéi Tsiyón*,[2] the Lovers of Zion, burning with the

---

[1] Some, however, hold that all such prophecies were fulfilled when the Jews returned to Jerusalem from Babylon.

[2] The conventional spelling "Choveve Zion" gives a false impression to the English reader.

love of Zion, *Hibbáth Tsiyón*—to behold her face before they died. Disraeli, the first imperialist, wielding an Empire, creating an Empress, still yearned in his heart and cried in his lyric romance for Zion.[1] Before the end of his century there arose a giant in Israel, splendid to look upon as the bearded and winged deities of Assyria. The scandal of Dreyfus convinced Theodor Herzl that there was no refuge for the soul of Jewry, either from martyrdom or assimilation into nothing, save an individual land, state, and name: *die letzte Anstrengung der Juden.* What other land could there be than *Eretz Yisroel,* the Land of Israel? The spirit of world Jewry was moved by the grand conception, as the spirit of modern Greece used to be moved by the Μεγάλη 'Ιδέα—the Great Idea—of Constantinople, only more profoundly and far more justifiably; for the supreme intellects of Athens had lived and died five hundred years before the Roman built Constantinople, whereas the creative spirit of Judaism was of The Land, and ceased to create when The Land was taken from them. Therefore this Austrian Jew, Theodor Herzl, was able to stand before the Sultan of Turkey, empowered to buy back from him Palestine for the Jews. But that tremendous boon which the Sultan might have granted, the Caliph, fearing the anger of his Moslem Empire, refused; and once more hope seemed to die. There were already projects for colonization in South America when Joseph Chamberlain, the greatest Secretary of State of the greatest Colonial Empire, had the vision to offer Zion in exile a healthy, fertile and beautiful territory in East Africa. For many, including Herzl himself, the quest seemed to be ended; and the offer would have been accepted but for a small group headed by one

[1] In *Tancred* (1847) a Jerusalem Jew says: "The English will take this city; they will keep it." It is not unreasonable to assume that in securing Cyprus for Great Britain he felt that, sooner or later, the step would bring Palestine and Syria within the orbit of British Control.

strong Russian with the face and the determination of
Lenin himself, and with Zionism coursing in his blood.[1]
I remember Chaim Weizmann asking me as in a parable
whether a band of Englishmen, banished for many
years all over the world, would accept as a substitute
for home permission to "return" to Calais: so felt he
and his for the prospect of Zion in Uganda. Uganda
was rejected, and Weizmann became a Lecturer in
Chemistry at the University of Manchester, then in the
constituency of Arthur James Balfour. The statesman
whose heart was in science would take refuge from party
routine with a scientist whose soul was in politics; and
the first seeds of sympathy were sown. With the War
came a demand for high explosives only less imperative
than that for human lives, and Acetone, an essential
ingredient of Trinitrotoluol—T.N.T.—was found to be
unprocurable outside Germany. Its absence appalled
the British Admiralty, but not the brain of the Jewish
chemist. At his word the school-children of the United
Kingdom were seen picking up horse-chestnuts by
millions, and the Acetone famine ceased. Weizmann
subsequently registered but did not press his claim for
the invention, which was, on the skilful pleading of Sir
Arthur Colefax, honoured, though none too generously,
by the British Government.

But Acetone had registered another claim far more
precious to the inventor; and the name and proposals
of Weizmann and his colleagues, strongly supported
by Arthur Balfour, Herbert Samuel and Mark Sykes,
penetrated to the Supreme Council of the Nation and
of the Allies.[2] On 2 November 1917, one week before

[1] "Herzl gratefully accepted the Uganda scheme and submitted
it for ratification by Congress in 1903. . . . The Seventh Congress
1904 . . . decided not to embark upon the Uganda adventure.
. . . Herzl died of a broken heart in 1904." Lord Melchett, *Thy
Neighbour*, 1936.

[2] I am speaking figuratively, and agree that "Mr. Lloyd George
is not quite accurate in describing British policy in Palestine as
a kind of *quid pro quo* for the patriotic action of the Zionist

the expected fall of Jerusalem, despite two formidable oppositions — British Jewry, preferring to remain "hundred per cent. Englishmen of 'non-conformist' persuasion", and an India Office ultra-Islamic under a Jewish Secretary of State[1]—there was launched upon the world the momentous and fateful Balfour Declaration. By this instrument Lord Rothschild, bearer of the most famous name in world Jewry, was informed that "His Majesty's Government view with favour the establishment in Palestine of a National Home for the Jewish people and will use their best endeavours to facilitate the achievement of that object, it being understood that nothing shall be done which may prejudice the civil and religious rights of existing non-Jewish communities in Palestine, or the rights and political status enjoyed by the Jews in other countries". Mere promulgation by the British Cabinet of such a pronouncement would have been useless without the support of the principal Allies. Dr. Weizmann was fortunate indeed in his colleague Dr. Nahum Sokolow,[2] who obtained the adoption of the Declaration both from the French and Italian Governments, as well as from the Vatican, in letters addressed by those Governments to him personally; thus insuring its acceptance by the Peace Conference at Versailles. And it was Sokolow who as Head of the Zionist Delegation pressed for the British Mandate for Palestine.

The Declaration enjoyed an excellent Press, together with general and generous support from thousands of Anglican priests, Protestant ministers, and other religiously-minded persons throughout the Western Hemisphere; only the Central Powers bewailing their

---

leader. The Balfour Declaration was not part of a bargain, nor a reward for services rendered." Blanche Dugdale, *Arthur James Balfour*, p. 226n.
[1] Edwin Montagu.
[2] See *Orientations*, p. 403.

own delay in promulgating a similar document and the Church of Rome indicating early though not immediate reserve. In the numerous British constituencies enjoying a Jewish vote the Declaration was a valuable platform asset, and there was good reciprocal publicity in the almost apocalyptic enthusiasm telegraphed by politicians of standing to the Zionist Organization.

Behind the adoption of so novel a thesis by the most level-headed Cabinet in the world on the recommendation of a Russian Jew, there were alleged to lurk other considerations than mere eagerness for the fulfilment of Old Testament prophecy. British espousal of the Hope of Israel would, it was hinted, serve triply our interest as well as our honour by ensuring the success of the Allied Loan in America, hitherto boycotted by anti-Russian Jewish Finance; by imparting to the Russian Revolution, of which the brains were assumed to be Jewish, a pro-British bias; and by sapping the loyalty of the Jews fighting in scores of thousands on and behind the front of Germany. We may record with relief that even if these material inducements had influenced the decision, the Balfour Declaration was on results utterly clean from such profit.[1] The American Loan went much as had been anyhow expected; no sympathies for Britain accrued from the Soviets (which shortly denounced Zionism as a capitalist contrivance); and the loyalty of German Jewry remained unshaken— with the subsequent reward that the world is now contemplating.

In spite then of non-Zionist and anti-Zionist Jews, world Jewry was at last within sight of home. No

---

[1] "As late as January 1918, our Ambassador in Washington reported, on the authority of Mr. Justice Brandeis himself, that the Zionists 'were violently opposed by the great capitalists, and by the Socialists, for different reasons'. This in itself shows how baseless was the idea, once very prevalent, that the Balfour Declaration was in part a bargain with American financiers." Blanche Dugdale, *Arthur James Balfour*, p. 231.

more would an infinitesimal minority out of all her sixteen millions creep to Jerusalem for the privilege of being allowed to die on sufferance as in a foreign country. No longer would the Jews remain a people without a land, in exile everywhere; Consuls of the Spirit, bearing witness among aliens to the invisible glories of a vanished kingdom.[1] Civilization had at last acknowledged the great wrong, had proclaimed the word of salvation. It was for the Jews to approve themselves by action worthy of that confidence: to exercise practically and materially their historic "right". The soil tilled by their fathers had lain for long ages neglected: now, with the modern processes available to Jewish brains, Jewish capital and Jewish enterprise, the wilderness would rejoice and blossom like the rose. Even though the land could not yet absorb sixteen millions, nor even eight, enough could return, if not to form The Jewish State (which a few extremists publicly demanded), at least to prove that the enterprise was one that blessed him that gave as well as him that took by forming for England "a little loyal Jewish Ulster" in a sea of potentially hostile Arabism.

The mainspring of the Zionist ideal being the establishment of a Hebrew nation, speaking Hebrew, upon the soil of the ancient Hebrews, an urgent though unpublished item in the duties of the Commission was to produce certain *faits accomplis* creating an atmosphere favourable to the project (and stimulating to financial supporters) before the assembly of the Peace Conference. Early in 1918 the twelve foundation stones—to every tribe a stone—of the Hebrew University were formally

---

[1] Spiritual Zionism on unterritorial lines had henceforth no more bitter enemy than the practical Zionist. "*Bogéd, bogéd*— Traitor", exclaimed a Rabbi, when I mentioned to him (on a Cunard tender) the name of the famous Hebrew writer Achad Haām; "*Tziyoní ruhní—spiritual* Zionist !"

laid in the presence of a distinguished gathering which
included the Commander-in-Chief. The intrepid Commissioners soon advanced (to our admiring sympathy)
upon the organization of the Jewish Community, not
without a measure of success. The exclusive use of the
Hebrew language was imposed upon Jews with a
severity sometimes irritating to others, sometimes indeed
comic, but in my opinion entirely justified in theory
and by results. It was perhaps vexing for a tax or rate
collector who had heard a Jewish householder conversing
with a Moslem friend in good Arabic to be informed
that the speaker knew Hebrew only, and could not understand (or accept) a receipt printed and verbally explained
in Arabic. But in this and many other matters Zionism
was only applying the Turkish proverb *Aghlama'an
choju'a sud vermezler* ("To the not-crying child they
give no milk") and thereby accelerating the tentative
processes of the Military Administration. Again, a
fervent Zionist from Central Europe or America might
be daunted if his platform "message" in Yiddish was
greeted and drowned by howls of "*Dabér Ivrit*"—
"Speak Hebrew!" I myself was puzzled when, inspecting
a Zionist Dental Clinic, I asked a man, whose face I
thought I knew, what was wrong with him. To my
surprise he signified in Hebrew that he could not
understand me. The secretary of the Clinic was called
from the room, when the patient added in a hurried
undertone: "I've a terrible toothache, but if I say so
in anything but Hebrew I shan't be treated for it."
The anomaly was heightened by the absolute refusal
of the orthodox Rabbis to converse in anything but
Yiddish, reserving the holy language for sacred purposes.
Many Gentile residents and most visitors derided this
drastic revival of Hebrew, asking: "How far will
Hebrew take a Jew? Not even as far as Beirut"; and
only tolerating it on the explanation that it must entail
a rapid diminution of the German language, *Kultur* and

influence.[1] But what other language could a Jewish national revival in Palestine have adopted?

Dr. Weizmann further attempted an enterprise whose success would have been so dramatic as to exalt the horn of Zionism with joy and honour throughout the world. The Wailing Wall of Jerusalem is geographically the Western Wall—*Ha-Kotél ha-Maáravi*—of the Háram al-Sharíf—The Noble Sanctuary. Structurally and archaeologically the Wall is the Western Wall of the Temple Area, founded on nine courses of massive undressed blocks laid by Herod, some perhaps even by Zerubbabel and Solomon; and four higher courses of Roman or Byzantine masonry completed by eleven of Saracenic, of Turkish, even of nineteenth-century construction. Legally and juridically it is a portion of the surface of the Háram and, as such, the absolute property of the Moslem Community. Historically, the most famous wall in the world; spiritually, the heart of Israel. The Wall is subtended to the west by a strip of pavement some six yards deep which, together with some grey stone hovels and paths on a space a little deeper than a square described on the length of the Wall, constitutes the Jerusalem section of the Abū Mádian Waqf, a pious bequest dating from the reign of Nur al-Din, suzerain of Saladin, in favour originally of Moroccan pilgrims now become residents.[2] The Wailing Wall is the one sacred place left to the Jews from their former glory, and the custom of praying there extends at least back to the Middle Ages. It is to this ancient wall that the hearts of Orthodox and indeed of universal Jewry

[1] The battle between German and Hebrew in Palestine was fought out before the War and lost by the *Hilfsverein der Deutschen Juden*, a German Jewish society for the assistance of Jews in the East, which advocated the use of German in the Schools.

[2] The documents proving undisputed ownership are preserved by the Shaikh al-Magharba—Shaikh of the Moroccans, the *Mutawalli* or Guardian of this Waqf and of the "Tomb of Abú Mádian" hard by, and are registered in the books of the Moslem Court in Jerusalem.

turn from all over the world, especially upon the eve
of Sabbath, during Passover, the Jewish New Year,
the Day of Atonement, and the 9th of the month of
Āb, the traditional date of the destruction of the first
and third Temples. Such is the strength and continuity
of the tradition that the Jews may be said to have
established an absolute and acknowledged right of
free access to the Wall for the purposes of devotion at
any hour of the day or night throughout the year, for,
though it is sometimes asserted by Moslems that they
could legally erect a wall debarring public approach, no
Mandatory Government could countenance so flagrant
an infringement of the *Status quo*. On the other hand,
the Jewish right is no more than a right of way and of
station, and involves no title, expressed or implied, of
ownership, either of the surface of the Wall or of the
pavement in front of it. Dr. Weizmann proposed that
he should acquire this precious space for Jewish worship;
not indeed by purchase (for Waqf property may not be
sold), but by the lawful and frequent practice of exchange
against some other acreage. He offered to expend
£75,000, which sum was to include the rehousing of the
occupants, and he was prepared if necessary to raise his
offer much higher. I was instructed to examine and
report upon this proposal. I attached, and still attach,
no more sanctity to the Abū Mádian than to any other
Waqf: I was prepared rigorously to control any future
building there: it seemed improbable that the Jews
would desire to cheapen or to desecrate the surface of
their holiest place, and the balance of the money could
be devoted to the cause of Moslem Education. I
therefore supported the project before Clayton and
General Money,[1] both of whom approved it. Haddād
Bey[2] was of opinion that the chances of acceptance were

[1] Who succeeded Clayton as Chief Administrator of O.E.T.A.(S.).
See *Orientations*, p. 371.
[2] Christian Orthodox Syrian Chief of Police and advisor on
Arab affairs. See *Orientations*.

anyhow small, and would be infinitesimal if the offer came direct from the Zionists; I therefore consented to open the negotiations myself. I subsequently received a petition of protest from a representative body of leading Arabs, and, towards the end of September, found the general delicacy of the situation so greatly increased by parallel and unauthorized negotiations, which had been simultaneously opened by the Jews without my knowledge (or that of Dr. Weizmann), that on the urgent advice of Haddād I was compelled to recommend that the project should be abandoned. There can be no doubt that he was right. Even if the Mufti had been willing himself, he would have had to reckon with the quivering sensitiveness of his own public (quite apart from their growing fear of Zionism) over the slightest rumour of interference even with the ground adjoining the outside of the walls of the Háram al-Sharīf.[1] The acceptance of the proposals, had it been practicable, would have obviated years of wretched humiliations including the befouling of the Wall and pavement and the unmannerly braying of the Mufti's tragi-comic Arab band during Jewish prayer and culminating in the horrible outrages of 1929.

If after waiting for nearly two thousand years an impetuous people are suddenly informed that they may return home, they will arrive pardonably keyed-up to expectation of high immediacies; and it was from the Zionist point of view one of the ironies of the situation that something seemed to prevent the Government from granting them, not only the barren approaches to the Wailing Wall, but apparently anything else picturesque enough to arouse the enthusiasm of universal Jewry. Dr. Weizmann offered to procure several hundred mechanical ploughs, and so by the autumn of 1918

---

[1] The Parker excavations of 1910–11 *within* the Area (a very different matter) had provoked an explosion of indignation all over Turkey.

to provide wheat and barley for the needs of the British Army: the offer was refused. One of the first outward and visible signs of nationhood is a national flag. Thousands of light blue and white flags and banners mounting the shield of Solomon had been prepared joyfully to float over houses or wave in triumphal processions: almost immediately they provoked such a commotion that their use had to be virtually prohibited. The Zionist National Anthem *ha-Tiqvah* when played before a mixed audience produced awkwardness some-times resulting in untoward incidents.[1] Everywhere was a sense of frustration, hope deferred, promise cheated of performance.

If this disenchantment had been merely negative, "still we have borne it with a patient shrug". But that within the first decade of their charter Jewish blood should four times have stained their soil and that none of the rulers —so few, it seemed, of the murderers—should be held to account, added fierce anger to the bitterness of death. If their lawful defenders could not or would not defend them from treacherous assault, who could blame them for the secret collecting of arms to defend themselves?

The great adventure of Zionism soon drew upon itself, not necessarily from those most concerned, a withering fire of cheap and ill-informed criticism. At a time when Jews all over the world were pouring their money into Palestine, without hope of material return or even of beholding the country, wiseacres knew that "there must be money in it somewhere, or the Jews would not be going there". The Army riddle—"What is a Zionist?" "A Zionist is a Jew who is prepared to pay another Jew to go and live in Palestine"—was based on the supposition that the movement was financed by millionaires, whereas it was, in truth, mainly dependent upon the yearly shekel of the uncounted poor. Who again had ever heard of those sedentary stockbroking

[1] See *Orientations*.

Jews really consenting to the dull physical toil of labouring on the land?—as if a race debarred for two thousand years from holding one acre could be expected without opportunity to give proof of deep love of the soil; as if the thousand deaths by malaria of the pioneers in marshes and dunes had no significance, any more than the young European graduates ploughing the plain of Sharon or breaking stones on the parched high-roads of Galilee.[1] Who that descended with Sir Herbert Samuel for the first Blessing of the New Vintage in *Rishón-le-Tsiyón*—First into Zion—and saw the proud skill of the harvesters and the tears of holy joy in the eyes of the older men when the British High Commissioner read the portion of the Law in Hebrew, could dare to doubt their physical energy or their worship of their land? It was not from lack of bodily prowess but from excess of individual skill that the Maccabean Football teams were defeated, though narrowly, by British Regiments; whilst in the Police Boxing Championships the Jewish Constables inflicted upon their Arab comrades a punishment bravely endured but so severe as to be almost more painful for the spectators. Recruiting for the Jewish Regiments, though good in the Palestine Colonies, had indeed elicited a poor response in the East End of London; but once in the

---

[1] "We are too liable to think of the Jews in those times just like the Jews of mediaeval and pre-emancipation times—people addicted peculiarly to finance and usury, with little aptitude, or rather opportunity, for agriculture and war. It was in Christian Europe, after so many walks had been shut to them, that the Jews betook themselves on a large scale to the handling of money, and developed those exceptional capacities which some people suppose to inhere in the Jewish nature as such. In the ancient world the Jews had no special reputation as financiers or usurers. Josephus, at the end of the first century A.D., was able to write —he was speaking of the Jews of Palestine—'We are not a commercial people; we live in a country without a seaboard and have no inclination to trade.' If you put together all the things said against the Jews in the remains of Greek and Latin anti-Semitic literature, you never find that they are attacked as usurers." *The Legacy of Israel*, p. 35. (Oxford University Press, 1927.)

east end of the Mediterranean the 38th, 39th, 40th and
42nd Battalions, Royal Fusiliers—Jordan Highlanders
as they were inevitably called—speedily disproved by
their fighting qualities the facetiously applied motto of
" No advance except on security". A British General
commanding one of the detachments which took Jerusalem told me at the time that the most reckless bravery
he had ever seen was shown by a young Jewish lance-
corporal of a London Regiment who, mounting over
a ridge into sudden sight of Jerusalem, seemed to be
transported and transformed, rushed alone against a
Turkish machine gun, killed the entire crew, and
captured the gun. Equally unfair, indeed wilfully blind,
is the tendency even now of those who concentrate upon
Arab grievances or the mistakes of individual Zionists,
and ignore the magnificent dedication of heart and brain,
of strength and strain, of time and treasure lavished by
World Zionism upon the Land of their soul's desire.

Is this, finally, a time for the Mandatory of the Nations
to show herself laggard or ungenerous in offering not
mere sympathy but their destined and appointed refuge
to the helpless victims of that pogrom of Central Europe
which is compelling the horror and indignation of the
civilized world ?

For the contrary opinion about Jews and land-tenure:
"It is true that Jewish migrations in historic times have often
been provoked by persecutions, but the question remains whether
the original nomadism brought about by geographical reasons has
not been just as determining a factor as the political-religious
factor in shaping the Jew's wandering life. We note large Jewish
migrations in the middle of the sixteenth century (the Jewish
migration towards eastern Europe), and in the nineteenth century
(the Jewish migrations to America).

"The nomadic habits of the Jews have also to do with the fact
that the Jewish race has not been able to attach itself to the soil,
has not been able to build states of its own. Does it not say in
Leviticus: 'And the land shall not be sold in perpetuity; for the
land is mine: for ye are strangers and sojourners with me'?"
Ragnar Numelin, Ph.D., *The Wandering Spirit*, p. 287. (Macmillan
and Co., 1937.)

II

But when the chosen People grew more strong,
The rightful cause at length became the wrong;
And every loss the men of Jebus bore,
They still were thought God's enemies the more.
Thus, worn and weaken'd, well or ill content,
Submit they must to David's Government.

JOHN DRYDEN, *Absalom and Achitophel*

The thesis of Zionism had been in part upheld by the general ignorance of the nature and conditions of Palestine; which was vaguely imagined as consisting of hills far away but green until the destruction of the Temple by Titus A.D. 70, after which they reverted to Desert, still potentially fertile, though practically uninhabited. It was assumed that the indigenous population of Palestine was small, " backward "[1] and unimportant: that as brother Semites, they would welcome Jews, and as poor men, capitalists: that somehow their interests would not only not suffer but would positively be advanced by an influx of enthusiastic and energetic "kinsmen": that they must realize the Jews were "returning" by the will of the League of Nations. (It was further presumed by average cynical opinion that none of the fifty-two signatories were going to quarrel with their Jews over so remote and objective an issue—to say the least were not going to retain them against their will: "Let My People go?" "Yes verily, and by God's help so I will!") The Palestinian opposition to Zionism therefore came on the whole as a surprise, sometimes almost as an outrage, to the world at large. An act of chivalrous generosity (at no expense to the Donors) was being heckled and thwarted by a selfish, petulant and fanatical reaction.

[1] As it had in fact been before the intensive arrival of the European Christians towards the end of the nineteenth century.

Not all this opposition was unreasonable or re-
actionary. For four centuries the Arabs, Moslem as
well as Christian, of Syria and Palestine (one country
though administratively divided into two),[1] had groaned
under the heavy empty hand of Ottoman misrule. After
the Young Turk Revolution in 1908 the grasp had
seemed for a while to lighten, but too soon the Arabs
found that though forms might alter, facts remained
unchanged—that even now they were denied the official
use of the noble Arabic language. For the generation
before the War a hope had arisen. The gaze of Syria
was bent on the South-west, where across the Sinai,
barely one hundred miles away, shone before them
another ancient country, restored to prosperity and
endowed with the civilization of Europe by the power
of Great Britain and the genius of an Englishman.[2]
The English yoke in Egypt, compared with that of the
neighbouring Powers elsewhere, seemed in Syrian eyes
easy and uninterfering. A national Sovereign sat on
his throne, assisted by a Council of Egyptian Ministers,
against a background of parliamentary institutions.
No attempt was being made to impose the English at
the expense of the Arabic language or culture, or to
manipulate the Customs tariffs for the benefit of
British trade.[3] For Syrians the hope had been that

[1] Owing to the number and delicacy of international problems
in Jerusalem, the Mutasárref, or Governor of Judaea, corresponded
directly with Constantinople, and not through the Vali of Syria,
though Palestine and Syria were one military command.

[2] Evelyn Baring, Lord Cromer.

[3] This British fairness of outlook in the matter of contracts is
well seen in the reply to the protests of the British Boilermakers,
Iron and Steel Ship-builders and Gas-holder-makers Society when
the contract for a Nile Bridge was adjudicated to the *Fives Lill*
Company because of their £18,000 lower tender. "It is impossible
for the British Government to do more, in connection with the
placing of orders by the Egyptian Government, than to give all
the assistance they properly can to the representatives of British
Firms who offer tenders, and to see that no unfair preference
is given to others." This attitude was appreciated by Egyptians:

after the next war Britain would expel the Turks and do for Syria what she had done for Egypt. Syrian politicians in Cairo had frequently endeavoured to interest the British Representative in their grievances and aspirations, but, in deference to French views about Syria, they had never been received, officially or un-officially (a refusal which did not always prevent some of them from resting a while in the Residency garden and then reporting to their colleagues outside the gates —and sometimes to the Representative of France— that they had enjoyed a most encouraging interview).

The next War came. The Arabs of the Hejaz received, early and unasked, assistance, arms and unconditional independence. Though British forces crossing the Sinai and advancing into Palestine met with no active military co-operation from Arabs (for Lawrence's Arabs were not from Palestine, and the Turks had broken up their Arab Regiments to distant fronts);[1] though the passive resistance of the civil population to the Turks was worth almost nothing to the advancing army; nevertheless, Syrian Arabs of influence had paid with their lives for their Allied sympathies, when a score of them was executed at Beirut, and when the Mufti of Gaza was hanged, together with his son, at the Jaffa Gate of Jerusalem.[2] With the British "Liberation" of their country they found their hopes not accomplished but extinguished. Throughout history the conqueror had kept for himself the territory he con-quered (save in those rare instances where he returned it to the inhabitants); and that Britain should take and

by Rival Powers not believed—and understandably, for which of *them* would have acted thus?

[1] Except the 27th Arab Division which distinguished itself in the first successful defence of Gaza 1917, and which was the last recruited largely in Palestine.

[2] My Arab orderly said: "He was a good man, greatly respected; therefore we all assembled to see him hanged."

keep Palestine would have been understood and welcomed. Instead she proposed to hand it, without
consulting the occupants, to a third party; and what
sort of third party! To the lowest and (in Arab eyes)
the least desirable specimens of a people reputed para-
sitic by nature, heavily subsidized, and supported by
the might of the British Empire. If the Jews were "not
coming but returning" to Palestine—the distinction
sounded verbal[1]—on the strength of a Book written
two thousand years ago; if there were no international
statute of limitations and the pages of history could be
turned back indefinitely, then let the Arabs "return"
to Spain,[2] which they had held quite as long and at least
as effectively as the Jews had held Palestine. That it
was the Book that counted, that Arab Spain meant
nothing to the world beyond two or three palaces and
a few Spanish derivations, whereas Palestine of the
Hebrews meant the Legacy of Israel, could hardly be
expected to appeal to Moslem or Christian Arabs of
Palestine as a justification for their ultimate subjection
or submersion.[3]

[1] Even with the authority of Aeschylus:

AIΣ.   ἥκω γὰρ ἐς γῆν τήνδε καὶ κατέρχομαι,
ΕΥ.   δὶς ταυτὸν ἡμῖν εἶπεν ὁ σοφὸς Αἰσχύλος.
AIΣ.   οὐ δῆτα τοῦτό γ' ὦ κατεστωλμυμένε
ἐλθεῖν μὲν εἰς γῆν ἔσθ' ὅτῳ μετῇ πάτρας·
χωρὶς γὰρ ἄλλην συμφορὰς ἐλήλυθεν·
φεύγων δ' ἀνὴρ ἥκει τε καὶ κατέρχεται.

AESCH.   For I am come returning to this Land.
EUR.   Our clever Aeschylus has said the same thing twice.
AESCH.   It's not the same, you blabber.
A man "comes" to his country when he has never been
banished,
For he simply comes without any misfortune implied,
But an exile both "comes" and "returns".
Aristophanes, *Frogs*, ll. 1022 . . . (B.C. 405), tr. Lucas
and Cruso.

[2] Or the Welsh to England.
[3] That the Arabs had "achieved" nothing in Palestine was
undeniable—though the new and interesting doctrine that the

The setting-back of the political clock set minds also back into fanaticisms, dying and better dead altogether. In the excitement of the "Holy Fire", the Shabāb—the Arab Young Men—would chant (for the Passion of Christ is still vivid in that heart of Christendom):

" Sabt al-Nur 'ayyídna	"The Sabbath of Light is our Festival
Wa zurna qabr Sayyídna.	And we have visited the tomb of Our Lord.
Sayyidna Aisa al-Massih	Our Lord is Jesus the Messiah;
W'al-Massih atāna	The Messiah has come to us,
B'dammu ishtarāna	With His blood He bought us;
Nahna al-yom farāha	We are to-day rejoicing
W'al-Yahud Hazzāna."	And the Jews are mourning."

Moslems, though everywhere more tolerant of Jews, not only as Ahl al-Kitāb, People of the Book, but also as "fellow-monotheists", than of Christians, nevertheless revered Jesus as *Rūh Allah*, the Spirit of God. Moslems as well as Christians would protest—"What ! hand our country over to the people who crucified Our Lord Jesus, *illi salabū Sayyídna Ísa !*"

Arab disappointments over the fact of the National Home were far from being allayed by the manner of its

---

inhabitants of a country can only retain it by proof of "achievement" seems hardly that of self-determination. What was an Arab to think when his title to the soil was publicly questioned by Jews? As it still is: "It is obvious that the Arabs have not the slightest historical claims to the possession of Palestine. Their only claims are the claims of people inhabiting the Land for centuries past. . . ." M. Edelbaum, 3 July 1936 (letter to *Great Britain and the East*).

Palestine, 23 Sept. 1936, thus disposes of the title to the soil based on a mere 1200 years' continuous occupation: "The doctrine, put forward as something like a sacred dogma, appears to be that any people who at any time happen to find themselves in control of an area are eternally entitled to its exclusive possession, no matter what contribution they fail to make and succeed in preventing others making to the cause of humanity and civilization."

c

announcement. The Declaration which, in addition to
its main Jewish message, was at pains to reassure non-
Palestinian Jews on the score of their national status,
took no account whatever of the feelings or desires of
the actual inhabitants of Palestine. In its drafting,
Arabs observed the main and positive portion to be
reserved for the Jewish people, while the other races
and creeds already in Palestine were not so much as
named, either as Arabs, Moslems or Christians, but
were lumped together under the negative and humiliating
definition of "Non-Jewish Communities" and relegated
to subordinate provisos.[1]   They further remarked a
sinister and significant omission. While their religious
and civil rights were specifically to be safeguarded, of
their political rights there was no mention whatever.
Clearly, they had none.

These and other suspicions and apprehensions were
brought to a head and manifested definitely for the first
time on the arrival of the Zionist Commission,[2] explana-
tions and justifications for which were received with
growing incredulity. The Arabs felt that the Commission was the thin end of the wedge, the beginning
of a Government within a Government. They were
not alone in this interpretation. In order to keep in
close contact with Jewish affairs, I had appointed an
able young Jew as Secretary, a position he had also held
for Dr. Weizmann. During my absence in Haifa I
heard from the acting Governor: "Cornfeld informed
me that he was instructed to make a report to the

[1] "What are the communities of Palestine? The reader of newspapers would answer, without hesitation, Arabs and Jews. Yet
the mandate contains no mention of an Arab community."
Survey of British Commonwealth Affairs, 1918–36, p. 434.

I remember the indignation of the Building, Roadmaking and
other Departments of the Public Works Ministry, Cairo, at being
budgeted as "Services other than Irrigation".

[2] Zionists, "*Tsiyōnim*", so light a Hebrew anapaest, became
in Arabic the two heavy uncompromising spondees *Sīhōnīyīn*.

Zionist Commission on the work in this office, but I stamped on that heavily and told him to send the report to me. He has done so, and I notice a proposal to establish a 'Jewish Bureau'." Here was no question of the hidden hand, of Secret Protocols of the Elders of Zion[1] or of any other criminal absurdity invented by anti-Semitism, but rather of a genuine misinterpretation of the degree of liaison that should subsist between an Official Administration and an officially-recognized Commission. Arab suspicions seemed to become certainties publicly verified by 1921, when the Moslem-Christian Delegation visited London seeking for further light upon the policy of His Majesty's Government, and were repeatedly recommended by the Colonial Office to get into touch with the Zionist Organization.[2]

Again, the pay of a clerk or a policeman sufficient for the Arab standard of living being considered insufficient for the European Jewish standard, Jewish policemen and clerks were being subsidized by the Zionist Commission; so, even in 1921, were railwaymen and telephonists. The Mayor of Jerusalem was assailed by demands to employ Jewish labour for road construction and repair: road labour, not being like Public Security a key position, received no Zionist subvention; if therefore the Mayor was to meet these demands, he must not only throw Arabs out of employment, but by paying their rivals higher wages materially raise his road bill and, in the end, the rates. Leading Jews in England were known to have the immediate ear of more than one Cabinet Minister: no Arab had. Hardly one

[1] Shortly to be exposed by Philip Graves in *The Times*, but still cited by Hitler, Nazis, and even by some educated people. See *The First Quarter*, p. 42.

[2] "But there is another aspect of the Jewish community, in which its relationship to the mandatory power might almost be termed that of an *imperium ex imperio*. This aspect is typified by the Jewish Agency." *Survey of British Commonwealth Affairs*, 1918–36, p. 458.

of the Commission could speak Arabic. On the other hand they and other Jews (far more than Arabs) knew English, which was necessarily the test language for service in the Administration.[1] What limit could there be to their influence when (in 1922) the celebration of the King Emperor's Birthday could in Palestine be postponed two days so that it should not fall upon the Jewish Sabbath? And this though it had been duly observed on the Moslem Friday in 1921. Would the date of the least important festival have been altered on account of the Moslem Friday?[2] If, in his indignation at such a change of date, the Arab absented himself from the Birthday celebrations, he would appear to be lacking in respect for a King whom on the contrary he regarded with veneration.

The official adoption in General Allenby's first proclamation of the Hebrew[3] language, with its gradual extension throughout Governmental and Municipal activities, naturally entailed an ever-increasing staff of Hebrew interpreters, translators, stenographers, typists, printers and administrative officers, all supported by the tax-paying majority, which contemplated un-edified the refusal of linguistic martyrs to part with cash against receipts in Arabic. For one reason or another

[1] I found this fear expressed in Rome on my visits of 1919 and 1922, during which last Cardinal X remarked that it was not the mass immigration elements in Zionism which alarmed him so much as the preponderating influence in Palestine which might be acquired by a comparatively small number of Jews occupying high positions. He said that in Hungary the proportion of Jews was only 5 per cent. of the population, but as high as 40 or 50 per cent. in the learned professions. This inclined him and others to be sceptical when they saw high official positions given so soon to Zionist Jews. I was at pains, on both occasions, to correct His Eminence on this point. Very few Jews, or Arabs, then held or now hold senior official positions.

[2] June 1922. It is of course true that rest on the Moslem Friday is permissive but on the Jewish Sabbath obligatory.

[3] Jewish Colonies on earlier Arab sites have naturally given them Hebrew names: the Arab thus sees some score of traditional Arab villages disappear from the map, and from official documents.

every circumstance or step taken to implement the Balfour Declaration[1] evoked a swelling chorus of protest against an admitted departure from the Laws and Usages of War. Between anxieties and suspicions the pitch of good relationship was being irreparably queered. Dr. Weizmann suggested to me that as a gesture of sympathy and friendliness he should present the Mufti with a Koran. I procured him a magnificent example from Cairo. The Mufti, preferring a private presentation, elected to accept the great manuscript unattended in his Office at the Moslem Law Courts. By that evening Arab Jerusalem had decided that the box taken into the room had in reality contained money.

The spirit of opposition throve in the unsettlement resulting from the inordinate delay in the promulgation of the Palestine Mandate, which, though officially awarded to Great Britain in April 1920, was, owing to difficulties with France, Italy and the Vatican, not signed until July 1922. Meanwhile Arab uncertainties had synchronized with those of President Wilson, who early in 1919 proposed[2] to the other Big Three that a Joint Allied Commission should be sent to enquire what would be the unfettered self-determination of the Ottoman Empire. The proposal could only have been acceptable to a person without knowledge of or interests in the Near East; but the Three agreed in principle, doubtless hoping to elude practice by subsequent defection. For once the President had thought ahead of his colleagues and had his way: the American members of the Commission started alone. Its Western

[1] And some that had nothing to do with it: "I had arranged for a Military Band to play on Saturdays in the Municipal Gardens, and I have to receive a deputation of leading Moslems who complain that their religion and their prestige are being undermined for the benefit and by the machinations of the Zionists (orders given that Band shall play until further notice on Fridays, Saturdays and Sundays)." (Letter to Mark Sykes.)

[2] On *Faisal's* adroit suggestion *v*, Antonius, *The Arab Awakening*, p. 287 *et seqq.*

wing, the King-Crane Commission, composed of two distinguished American statesmen, Dr. Henry C. King and Minister Charles R. Crane, forthwith descended upon O.E.T.'s East and West and South and North, and began to enquire from the various and opposed communities what were their political aspirations, thus appearing to reopen to appeal a *chose jugée* and so restarting the general unsettlement. Few that had the privilege of meeting Dr. King or of knowing the surviving Commissioner will be disposed to doubt that, though the hands that signed their Report were the hands of King-Crane, the voice was the voice of Crane. It appeared that from Cilicia to the borders of Egypt all tongues creeds and nations, save the Jews (who were for British Zionism) and the Roman Catholics (who were for France), desired as their first choice an American Mandate: failing which the vast majority favoured Great Britain. When it is remembered that to the anticipating Eastern mind the nationality of the Commission (apart from the known wealth and rumoured Liberalism of America) pre-determined that of the Mandatory, it will be understood that these findings were more favourable to Great Britain than would be gathered from a literal reading of their text. The Commissioners recommended a single Mandate for a united Syria, including Palestine (with a retarded Zionism) and the Lebanon; the Mandatory, failing America, to be Great Britain, with the Amir Faisal ibn Husain as Constitutional Monarch. In their dislike of any partition of United Syria they quoted W. M. Ramsay: "The attempt to sort out religions and settle them in different localities is wrong and will prove fatal. The progress of history depends upon diversity of population in each district."[1] The answer of the Immanent Will

[1] This Report, which was signed on 28 August 1919 and presented to the American Commissioners in Paris the following day, was, doubtless for the best of reasons, not published until the end

(returned through the Dynasts of Versailles) to these reasoned recommendations was, that within one year United Syria had been divided into two Mandates and Faisal expelled; and that within three years its Northern portion, the French Mandate, had been redivided into five separate territories, each complete with full machinery of government, under the (sixth) supreme government of a High Commissioner in Beirut.

The eagerness of the Arabs, North and South, for a United Syria (strongly supported by Faisal in Paris) was not merely anti-French or anti-Zionistic. Even had they obtained this, the career previously open to talent in the Ottoman Empire would have been reduced by two-thirds. Kiamil Pasha, a Cypriot villager, had been four times Grand Vizir. Abu l'Huda, an Arab of Aleppo, had as Astrologer to the Sultan wielded for years an even more absolute though far less honourable power. Mahmud Shawkat of Baghdad had become Grand Vizier as recently as 1908. The two Arab Pashas I found in Jerusalem had held positions of administrative responsibility in Arabia and in Mesopotamia. After the partition of Syria the leading Palestine Arabs, conscious, if not of "Hands that the rod of Empire might have swayed", at least of some ruling capacity, found their ambitions henceforth confined to subordinate or municipal functions, with preference given to two

---

of 1922, and even then unofficially in the *New York Times*. In a Confidential Annex "For the American People" the writers dealt with the "interference" and attempted influencing of the populations. While good enough to allow that a comparative minimum of these practices was reported in O.E.T.A.(S.) they nevertheless proceeded to quote rumours and unsubstantiated stories of "pressure" exercised at Jaffa and Gaza. All I can say is that I myself, having been asked by one or two Arabs once or twice what they should say, and having replied that they should tell the truth, refused to receive any more questioners, conveying to them this standard reply through a subordinate: nor do I believe that any officer in General Money's Administration acted otherwise.

foreign races, within a territory no larger than Wales. Not only for the talents was opportunity restricted: it was therefore no matter for surprise that the representatives of ancient families, whether associated with the Ottoman Government or as great landowners, should wage a consistent and resentful rearguard action against the passing of their ascendency. Is not History a record of the reluctance of aristocracies and oligarchies to relinquish their position or to share it, even with their own people? But to share it with foreigners! For foreigners the Central European Jews were to the Arabs of Palestine, despite the oft-quoted Semitic bond of language—foreigners in all the essentials of civilization, and mainly Western both in their qualities and their defects. *Identity* of language is a bond: a common linguistic origin of several thousand years ago is no more than an academic fact. Linguistic fellow-Semites might possibly be driven into alliance by a Mongol invasion, but when a Shaikh enquired how far Englishmen had acted upon their Indo-Germanic kinships during the past half-century, what was the answer? In default of the Semitic bond there survived, perhaps fortunately, no Canaanite tradition.

The injunction, under Article 6 of the Mandate, that the Administration "shall encourage in co-operation with the Jewish Agency close settlement by Jews on the land, including State lands and waste lands not required for public purposes" in Palestine, sounded with a curious difference in different ears. To the world at large it seemed a reasonable satisfaction by the bestowal of surplus, unused and unwanted areas. To the Zionist, who had hoped that with the prosperity of British rule his rapidly augmented population would need every possible acre of land in the country, it was the obvious initial minimum of concession unwarrantably delayed by the Government. The thinking Arabs regarded Article 6 as Englishmen would regard

instructions from a German conqueror for the settlement and development of the Duchy of Cornwall, of
our Downs, commons and golf-courses, not by Germans, but by Italians "returning" as Roman legion-
aries. For such loss of national and political future
repeated reassurances of strict and scrupulous maintenance of religious rights and sites (assumed under British
rule everywhere) were about as satisfactory compensa-
tion as would be German guarantees to Englishmen
for the inviolable conservation of the Court of Arches
and of Westminster Abbey. Article 6 has not yet been
"implemented", owing to the lack of available State
property, but it still stands in the Mandate, and is still
being vigorously pressed by Zionists. "The Jewish
Agency would appreciate an opportunity of examining
any Government lands still unallocated, with a view
to applying for any areas suitable for Jewish settlement."[1]
The resentment of leading Arabs increased when they
were pilloried in Zionist reports and the general literature based thereon as *Effendis*.[2] The Fellah, the peasant,
was a fine fellah, a stout fellah, with all the bluff and
blunt virtues conventionally ascribed to peasantry by
those who know it least. He was also unorganized and
inarticulate. The *Effendi* on the other hand was a
decadent "capitalist" parasite, a selfish obstructive
agitator of an Arab Majority not ill disposed if only
"left to themselves". His "small clique" of "feudal
gentry exploiters" was bound in the end to be "elimin-

[1] Dr. Weizmann's letter to the High Commissioner, covering
annual Memorandum to the League of Nations for 1935, 30 April
1936.
[2] Effendi is an early Turkish corruption of the Byzantine $αὐθέντης$,
an authentic, or gentleman. It corresponds to Mr. in conversation and to Esquire upon an envelope. Bey may be regarded as
the equivalent of a Knight or Baronet, and Pasha of a Peer. None
of the three is hereditary, though the son of a Pasha is a Bey
by courtesy. The Turks were chary in their creation. I found
but two in Palestine after the War, and in Transjordan one. Pashas
are addressed as "Excellency"; there are therefore more Excellencies
in one province of Egypt than in the whole British Empire.

ated" and so entitled to no quarter, even if some British officials chose to be taken in by his veneer of "cringing" good manners. *Effendis* in that sense of the word there certainly were and are throughout the Near and Middle East; in Palestine the *Effendi* might as a whole be defined as an Arab of the ruling or professional "black-coated" class, debarred from employment for political as well as for economic reasons. The *Effendi's* good will was not perceptibly stimulated by the theory that while the Arabs East of the Jordan were a splendid people and the real thing, those West of the Jordan were not Arabs at all but merely Arabic-speaking Levantines.[1]

Material advantages were admittedly increased for many, though not for all, Arabs, especially near the City and the towns. But at what a price! Was it altogether dishonourable for Arabs to sigh for a less advanced, but a traditional, an Arab civilization? The peasant of Siloam would not have been a peasant if he had not profited by being able to sell his cauliflower for sixpence instead of a halfpenny; the improvident landowner would have been more, or less, than human if he refused tenfold the value of his land. Yet both might mutter, in the words of the Palestine chicken: *At'emni al-yōm: w'ushnuqni bukra*—"Feed me up to-day: wring my neck to-morrow."

In spite—or because—of official glosses on the original text of the Declaration, Arabs seemed to understand less and less what, if any, were its limitations. It was said that though Dr. Weizmann's moderated demands at the Peace Conference went beyond what he considered sound, they were the minimum requisites of other prominent Zionists. On the King's Birthday of 1921 Sir Herbert Samuel pronounced a statesmanlike speech

---

[1] This ethnologically correct, but nationally misleading thesis, is also embodied in the Foreign Office *Handbook of Syria and Palestine*, pp. 56–7, 1920.

which reassured the Arabs, and the world. He defined the Declaration as meaning that "The Jews, a people who are scattered throughout the world, but whose hearts are always turned to Palestine, should be enabled to found here their home, and that some among them, within the limits that are fixed by the numbers and interests of the present population, should come to Palestine in order to help by their resources and efforts to develop the country, to the advantage of all its inhabitants." Within two months the good effect of the speech in Palestine was undone by its violent denunciation at the Carlsbad Zionist Congress. Herzl's original "Judenstadt"[1] was indeed absolutely and permanently excluded by the British Government as well as repudiated by official Zionism; but with the Revisionists, swayed by the versatile and violent Vladimir Jabotinsky,[2] declaiming publicly at the first Zionist Congress at The Hague that what the Jews really wanted was not a Jewish National Home, but a Jewish State, which of the three (if any) was an Arab to believe? All he knew was that in advanced politics the extremists of the past generation were the Liberals of the second and Conservatives of the third.[3] Above all, how could

[1] As long ago as 11 February 1899, "Glasgow Zionist" wrote to the *Speaker*: "Zionism does not even dream of founding a state for all Jews"—an equivocal repudiation.

[2] ". . . in those early years the work of fomenting discord was aided by the extravagant and provocative utterances of a small section of Zionists." Blanche Dugdale, *Arthur James Balfour*, p. 221.

[3] What, for instance, is the Arab reader to deduce from the following reasoned statement?: "It is an important feature of the peculiar character of the Palestine Mandate that while in all other cases it is the actual inhabitants of the countries in question who are the beneficiaries of the Mandates, under the terms of the Palestine Mandate, it is *the Jewish people as a whole* who are the beneficiaries jointly with the existing population of Palestine. This distinction is one of paramount importance, both in principle and fact. It means that while the rights of the Arabs are based on their residence in the country, the rights of the Jews are independent of this qualification, for the Trust being held by Great

he forget that when Dr. Weizmann was asked at the Peace Conference in Paris what he meant by the Jewish National Home, he had replied that there should ultimately be such conditions that Palestine should be just as Jewish as America was American, or England was English? [1]

Zionism is a world movement. Arabism does not exist. Although it is said that a knowledge of Arabic will take you from India to the Atlantic, yet Arab merits, defects, rights and grievances are essentially local in character, even when reinforced by the Vatican and by the relics of Pan-Islam. The Arab of Palestine therefore feels himself under an overwhelming inferiority in the presentation of his case to the conscience of the world.[2] He is aware that he has not the ability, the organization, least of all the material resources or the audience for effective propaganda. He is well aware that such of his leading Moslems as have toured the world for support have not succeeded in creating a favourable impression even upon their co-religionists in Egypt, India or Arabia. Against the scientifically controlled publicity of the two major continents he has about as much chance as had the Dervishes before Kitchener's machine guns at Omdurman. From time to time his cause is "taken up", usually with more courage than skill, by some English supporter (Thack-

---

Britain for the Jewish National Home to be established in Palestine for the benefit of the Jewish people, it does not depend on the numerical strength of the present Jewish population of Palestine. By virtue of this Trust any Jew no matter where he lives is a potential colonist and beneficiary of the Trust." J. M. Mackover, *Governing Palestine*, 1936.

[1] Israel Cohen, *Jewish Life in Modern Times*, p. 310.

[2] ". . . one further inequality. This was inequality of access to the ear of the British democracy. Jewry was represented in every layer of English society—in the Lords and the Commons, in powerful capitalistic organizations and in the Labour party, in the press and in the Universities." *Survey of British Commonwealth Affairs*, p. 462, 1918–36.

eray's "young Mr. Bedwin Sands"), too often a mere travelled *amateur* of picturesque survivals. In British politics Conservatives were at first inclined to be pro-Arab (with notable exceptions in the Upper House) and Liberals and Labour pro-Zionist. Politically, all the Arabs in the world would not have turned at the Polls one single vote. On the contrary, I have been asked by a Member as guest at a Party luncheon in the House of Commons, whether the Palestine Government were advancing as swiftly as possible with the National Home, "for," he said, "I have in my constituency some thousands of Jews who are continually enquiring, whereas," he added with engaging but unnecessary candour, "I have no Arabs."

All too soon feeling deepened down to primal instinct, which was fired by misguided and irresponsible agitators to outrage. But "have not the Jews been arming from the first, and later has not the Government allowed them, granted them, great cases of rifles? What they have beyond that who can know? But could any man believe that the beehives bursting with revolvers found by the English in the Haifa Customs were not one of a hundred more successful consignments?"[1] And with illicit arming who, the Arab asked, was the proved aggressor?

[1] "In October 1935 a mysterious munitions-transport arrived in Jaffa. The weapons were hidden in cement-sacks, addressed to an unknown Isaac Katan in Tel Aviv. When the cement-sacks were opened, the customs officers found 300 rifles, some 500 bayonets and 400,000 rounds of munitions in 359 of them. The discovery of this unfortunate merchandise led to demonstrations, gave rise to an embittered campaign in the whole Arab Press, and finally, on 26 October, resulted in a strike of protest in Jaffa. On this day the Arabs of Jaffa tried to attack Tel Aviv, but the Government still had the control tightly in its hands and dispersed the crowd.

"It was later revealed that the munitions-transport was not intended for the Jews, but belonged to a large smuggling syndicate which was trying to import weapons into Abyssinia in a roundabout way." Ladislas Farago, *Palestine on the Eve*.

III

Semper ego auditor tantum! Nunquamne reponam?[1]   JUVENAL I.

I have attempted to describe, I hope not without sympathy and justice, the aspirations of Zionism formulated
in the Balfour Declaration, endorsed by the League of
Nations, and interpreted by the Zionist Commission,
together with their repercussion upon the indigenous
Arabs of Palestine. Grappling with this situation was a
British Military Administration, the third, and ostensibly
directing party, confronted with a problem unique in
history; by some interpreted as the problem of how *A*
should "restore" the property of *B* to *C* without depriva-
tion of *B*. The mistakes and misfortunes in the handling
of this experiment were by no means confined to any
one, or any two, of these three suddenly assembled and
ill-assorted partners; nor can they be dissociated from
the Managing Directors in Downing Street or the fifty
apathetic shareholders meeting in Geneva. All concerned manifested with a frequency that seemed not
to decrease with years the "blank misgivings of a creature
moving about in worlds not realized". Almost from
the beginning O.E.T.A. incurred a critical Zionist
Press which soon developed into Pan-Jewish hostility.
We were inefficient, ill-educated; those with official
experience strongly pro-Arab, violently anti-Zionist,[2]
even anti-Jewish. Governing and governed had each
one clear advantage over the other, for if O.E.T.A.
officials could not be removed by Press agitation, they
were by a proper British convention precluded from
defending themselves in public; with the result that the

[1] "Always the auditor, and nothing more !" Gifford.
[2] "I attended an infinitely tedious Arab version of *Hamlet*
(title role addressed throughout as Shaikh *Hamlik*) concluding
with friendly references to Great Britain for having delivered the
Arabs from Turkish domination and total repression of the Arab

difficulties[1] they encountered on all sides are even now not generally appreciated.

The truth is that some (though by no means all) of the Zionist criticisms of our inefficiency might have been justifiable if they had been directed against a planned, trained and established Civil Service. But what was O.E.T.A.? It was the remnant of the small staff originally chosen for the purpose, with accretions of the officers placed by the Army in temporary charge of newly conquered areas: without expectation of long continuance, still less of permanency. And who were these officers? What had they been before the War? There were a few professional soldiers. Apart from these our administrative and technical staff, necessarily drawn from military material available on the spot, included a cashier from a Bank in Rangoon, an actor-manager, two assistants from Thos. Cook, a picture-dealer, an Army coach, a clown, a land valuer, a bo'sun from the Niger, a Glasgow distiller, an organist, an Alexandria cotton-broker, an architect (not in the Public Works but in the Secretariat), a Junior Service London Postal Official (not in the Post Office but as Controller of Labour), a taxi-driver from Egypt, two school-masters and a missionary. The frequency and violence of Jerusalem crises were such that "My Staff Capt. told me (of one of Percy's[2] successors) that he punctuated his work with groans, ejaculating 'The place is a night-mare, a *night*mare!'" Our three Chief

language, together with hope for the prosperity of the nation and the language. I had naturally to acknowledge these loyal and anti-Ottoman sentiments, and duly received a few days later an official protest from the Zionist Commission for having attended and encouraged anti-Zionist demonstrations (called for copies of speeches; nothing offensive found, discovered that proceedings were reported by a young Jew ignorant of the Arabic language)." (Early 1918 letter to Mark Sykes.)

[1] My recital of these difficulties is not to be taken as a general endorsement of O.E.T.A.

[2] Lord William Percy, my second and most efficient Deputy Military Governor. See *Orientations*.

Administrators were Generals changed (after the first appointment) too quickly to accomplish anything. The War Office and the Foreign Office between them provided neither precise instructions for policy nor trained administrators. Yet it would have been easy to appoint as Chief of Staff or Head of an Executive Secretariat some militarized Colonial or Chief Secretary—perhaps from Ceylon—familiar for a quarter of a century with the broad principles and technical minutiae of administration. Here indeed was our weakness, and for lack of this tradition and experience we doubtless expended much unnecessary time, tissue, and, I fear, money. Two sharp notes to Headquarters remind me how poor our liaison sometimes was.

Towards the end of last week a certain number of would-be Palestinian delegates and others interested in the question of a Palestinian Congress and a possible Palestinian Delegation to Europe visited me and informed me that they had had an interview with the Chief Administrator, who had recommended them to elect their delegates, and promised to facilitate their journey. As the only instructions in my hands were to the effect that the Palestinian Congress must not assemble, I was compelled to maintain a non-committal and even incredulous attitude. I would remark that the already great difficulties of Jerusalem politics are greatly increased for the Military Governor, unless he is kept continually and accurately informed of receptions and negotiations deeply affecting the public interest which are being carried on with the authorities by notables of his District in his District.

Again:

Shortly before noon yesterday I received telephonic information, confirmed later by your letter, to the effect that 300 Arabs of Abu Kish were proceeding by train and horseback to Jerusalem, and instructing me to

have them stopped both at the Station and on the
road at Kolonia. I therefore cut short an engagement
of long standing at Ramallah, got into touch with
O.C. Troops, who provided 30 men with lorries, Lewis
guns, rations, etc., for two days, and sent them with
all possible dispatch to Kolonia. I further arranged
with the Police for a representative of the Governorate,
with an interpreter, to be present both at the Station
and Kolonia. Both trains from Ludd were duly met;
the troops remained at Kolonia all night, and a picket
was posted on the Nablus Road in case the horse-
men should advance by way of Nebi Samwīl. Not a
single Arab of Abu Kish arrived by either of the trains
or on horseback. It would be interesting to know (a)
why, if the rumour was correct, the Arabs could not
have been dealt with at Ludd[1] and Ramleh[1] respectively,
and (b) if the rumour was false, what steps were taken
to verify or confirm it before inflicting upon the Governorate, local Police, and O.C. Troops, Jerusalem, this
apparently unnecessary expenditure of valuable time.

On the other hand, there was a high level of zeal,
goodwill, ability and interest in the task to hand; the
word "overtime" was unknown, and work ceased only
when it was finished. We tried by these efforts to atone
for admitted deficiencies, and I believe that the first
High Commissioner, with eleven years' experience of
Whitehall, found that we had not been altogether
unsuccessful.

The main charge against O.E.T.A., more serious
because it implied deliberate bad faith, was that of
anti-Zionism, It cannot be denied that there were
amongst us two or three officers in high positions overtly
against the declared policy of His Majesty's Government. In due course these were eliminated (for one
only saw fit to resign). One or two who would gladly

[1] Neither at that time in my district.

have remained in Mandatory Service became extreme
Arabists when discharged for reasons of economy.
While emphatically repudiating the general accusation
that O.E.T.A. was disloyal to its own Government,
we may yet allow that the more eager arrivals from
Central Europe were not altogether unjustified in arguing from these known examples to the possibility of
others unknown. They knew nothing of British Officers,
probably conceiving them as a variant of a Prussian
Drill Sergeant. They came from a country where the
official *Chinovnik* class lay awake at night excogitating
pogroms; where Father Gapon, the priest who led
hundreds of innocent men to be shot down, was but
one of innumerable state-paid *agents provocateurs*.
They found that while a good proportion of O.E.T.A.
(having come from Egypt) spoke Arabic, none as yet
knew Hebrew: hardly one, Russian or German. The
British were often seen conversing with Arabs; more
seldom with Jews. What more likely then that, so far
from calming the Arabs, they were encouraging their
opposition to the National Home?

Some of us were very soon on the Black List of Zion,
an injustice which though not prejudicing our work
did entail some needless irritation, as for instance when
I found myself publicly accused of having intentionally
caused the Wailing Wall negotiations to break down;
verifying, not for the last time, the Arab proverb that
"The peacemaker shall not profit, save in the rending
of his garments". On my first leave home in 1919 I
wrote to General Money: "Saw R. G. at the Foreign
Office, where Lord Curzon came in and told me of a
fierce attack made on me on the 2nd of the month by
the Commission, who stated openly that I ran an anti-
Jewish campaign during the three months of your
absence." Again, on my way back to Palestine I
"Lunched with Sokolow at the *Meurice* to meet Ussish-
kin, the great Russian Zionist. Good massive head,

but almost no French. Said he had heard nothing but discouraging reports from Palestine and that the Administration seemed to be *nettement* anti-Z.[1] I begged them to come out and see for themselves, and told them that the slow movers like myself were not only their best friends, but their only hope."[2]

The ardent Zionist from Pinsk or Przemysl, between the bitterly hostile Arab and the coldly impartial British official, always recalled to me Theocritus' description of Ptolemy, εἰδὼς τὸν φιλέοντα, τὸν οὐ φιλέοντ᾽ ἔτι μᾶλλον "Recognizing his friend, but his enemy even better"; sometimes indeed confusing the two. Jewish Doctors would alienate the Public Health Department even where their talents were most admired, and they seemed

---

[1] "In the early spring of 1918 Arab leaders in Palestine and Egypt were eager to come to terms with Zionists on the basis of mutual concessions. The Jews responded with the greatest readiness and cordiality. The Arabs' attitude grew more and more reserved, strictly parallel with the increasing antagonism of the British military administration to Zionism and Jewish claims. There are clear indications that in some cases direct advice was given to the Arab leaders . . . to abstain from concessions to the Jews. . . ."

"But notwithstanding this artificially-created antagonism on the spot between the local Arab leaders and the Jews of Palestine, the National Arab leadership, in their desire to foster the Arab national cause, were trying to enlist the help of the Jewish people by expressing their sympathy with the Zionist aims and willingness to collaborate with the Jews in the rebuilding of the Jewish National Home in Palestine."

" . . . Bitter enmity to Jewish national aspirations . . . vigorous, unscrupulous propaganda against the Jews . . .; unfortunately it found the sympathetic ear of the British authorities on the spot, who, for quite other reasons and considerations, were opposed to the Jewish aspirations."

From Political Report of the Zionist Organisation, quoted by J. M. Mackover, 1936.

Of these grave allegations some specific proof should be, but never has been, given. Is the world seriously asked to believe that the Palestine Arabs, so soon as they realized its implications, needed prompting and were not spontaneously opposed to political Zionism ?

[2] Before leaving for England I had written: "The Christian Communities have no idea of allowing Jerusalem to lose any of its prestige as the centre of the Christian religions, and are far from

to suffer (if that is the word) from a failure to appreciate
the point of view of the other man (Arab or British)
only equalled by that of their latest persecutors, the
German nation. Few writers have written more beauti-
fully or sympathetically about the Jewish people than
the brothers Jacques and Jérôme Tharaud. *L'Ombre
de la Croix* is a pathetic revelation which must have
immensely increased the volume and quality of interest
in Israel. Yet because (apparently) of their description
of Bela Kun in *Quand Israel est Roi*, the Editor of the
newspaper that had commissioned *Quand Israel n'est
plus Roi* was given the brusque alternative of suppressing
the later chapters or of losing his Jewish advertisements.

The British officer, work as he might, felt himself
surrounded, almost opposed, by an atmosphere always
critical, frequently hostile, sometimes bitterly vindic-
tive and even menacing. After the Easter riots of 1920
and the November riots of 1921 (before the mutual
spheres of responsibility between Governorate and
Police[3] had been properly defined), I had to endure
such a tempest of vituperation in the Palestine and World
Hebrew Press that I am still unable to understand how

---

sympathetic to my efforts to place the Jews in every way upon
an equality with the others."

Our intentions were better appreciated by Jews with a knowledge of the Near East. The Special Committee of Egyptian Jews,
Jack Mosseri, P. Pascal, Dr. Waitz, A. Alexander, for Relief of
Jews in Palestine, wrote to me on their return to Cairo: "to convey
to you its deepest thanks and gratitude for the reception accorded
to its delegates in Jerusalem, for the interest you showed in this
work, and for the arrangements made for them. We are deeply
sensible of the assistance you have given us, and we express the
appreciation not merely of ourselves and our afflicted brethren
in Jerusalem but of all Jewry. We should be happy to receive
from you any suggestions as to the method and progress of our
work."

One such word to any of us from official Zionism would have
shown, at the least, a recognition of our difficulties.

[3] During the Easter period of 1920 the Jerusalem Police Force
was, as stated in Ch. xiv of *Orientations*, under the command of
a junior Lieutenant.

I did not emerge from it an anti-Semite for life. The clamour indeed subsided so soon as it was clear that the British Government had no intention of yielding to it, and I think Jewry has since drawn its own conclusions from the succeeding five years of undisturbed peace in Jerusalem. After the Jaffa riots of May 1921, and most of all after the outbreak in 1929, the abuse of executive officers became proportionately louder and fiercer,[1] sparing only the thrice-blessed technician— the geologist, the bacteriologist and the veterinary surgeon. The British officer responsible for the Wailing Wall in 1928 received 400 abusive letters, from Jews all over the world. In agonies such as those who would not sympathise, who would expect a philosophic calm? Yet when I revisited Palestine in 1931, and found the British Administration fully convinced that in any future crisis, while the Arabs might be their enemies, the Jews certainly would be, I could not help asking myself how far these wild, derisive indignations could be said to have furthered the cause of Zion. However this may be (for my book is not written to criticize but to record— sometimes to speak for those who cannot speak for themselves), the Jews still detest, while the Arabs regret, though they often abused, the Military Administration.[2]

Visiting America a year or two later, I was struck

---

[1] "The Jews once more had a feeling that it was inconceivable this could have taken place against the wishes of the British officials." *Thy Neighbour*, p. 176.
Even this remarkable statement is as milk-and-water to the heroic denunciations of the time. Yet all these, and later troubles had been foreseen during the War by Talaat Pasha, himself a Dönmé, or crypto-Jew, who stated, in the interview with Count Bernstorf (quoted in his *Memoirs*): "I will gladly establish a National Home for the Jews, to please you, but, mark my words, the Arabs will destroy the Jews."

[2] Even in April 1936 the Palestine Officer of the Civil Government had the pleasure of reading that "The British Government in Palestine has great virtues, but sometimes one thinks of its unimaginative officialdom in terms of Bunyan's parable of the man who works, eyes cast down, with the muck-rake, and does

by the thoroughness with which the caricature of the British officer had been disseminated. Several American Jews expressed surprise that I was "not the same" as they had read in their newspapers. In 1934 a Jewish wheat magnate of Chicago told me that he had been to his amazement and disgust sharply rebuked by a travelling Zionist leader for attributing a measure of Palestinian progress to the British Administration. More recently I learnt that a Jewish lady who had left a British Dominion to settle in Tel Aviv was horrified by the stream of abuse poured there upon everything British. Such manifestations are what is called in Arabic *Kufr al-náamah*—"Denial of the Blessing", and certain it is that no blessing can attend them. Whatever our defects, I have yet to hear that the most virulent of these critics is able to suggest an acceptable alternative Mandatory. Still, these attacks had their uses. They taught one to keep one's temper. I find my only comment home on the general atmosphere was: "I do not want to end my career as a Ritual Sacrifice." They also drew British officers closer together. At the Armistice "Reunion Dinner" in 1921, when the speeches were over: "To my surprise I heard my name shouted aloud; and then a clapping, stamping and roaring which continued for two or three minutes. I recognized that this din was a definitely organized ovation of sympathy and protest against the attacks to which I have been subjected by the Jewish Press; and was so affected thereby that I could hardly reply." I believe my colleague Harry Luke was greeted with an even more significant demonstration at the St. Andrew's Dinner in 1929. Yet we both had plenty of British critics.

What made some of us think that we might not be

---

not see that someone is standing by and offering him a crown". *Palestine*, vol. XI, no. 10, p. 2.

The respective rôles of Briton and Zionist are no less tactfully than appetizingly contrasted.

wholly and always in the wrong was the relative lack of
success then enjoyed by the Zionist Commission with
considerable sections of local Jewry. Modern working
Zionism had its origin, certainly its mainspring, in
Russian Jewry, for which Britain was to provide and
America to furnish a National Home. If there was no
Herzl but Herzl, yet Weizmann was the prophet of
Herzl. The spirit of the living creed, predominantly
Russian, was reflected in the personnel, particularly
the permanent personnel of the Commission, and in the
outlook of the Commission not only upon the Administration but upon all the Sephardim of the Near East,
indeed upon all Jews other than the Ashkenazim from
the Northern and Central East of Europe. In England
we had known of the Sephardic or Spanish as the
"Noble" Jew. In the new land of Israel he was if not
despised at any rate ignored as a spineless Oriental.
Yet it was this same Eastern background that would
have rendered the Sephardim, had the Commission
deigned to employ their services, ideal agents for dealing
or negotiating with the Arabs, with whom they had
maintained a close and friendly contact ever since the
Expulsion from Spain in 1492.[1] Very soon I found
that my old friendship with the Egyptian Sephardi
families told, if at all, against me—and true it is that,
partly from the delicacy of their position in a Moslem
country, partly from lack of Zionist encouragement,
Egyptian Jewry had proved lukewarm to the Cause.
I found such as I was able to enlist invaluable.[2]

[1] (And from Portugal in 1497.) Sephardi Jews were established
in Spain before the Roman Emperors: and had materially assisted
the Arab conquest thereof.

[2] "Little more than a generation (after the Expulsion) saw a
Jewish community in Palestine some ten thousand in number,
with the influence and leadership in the hands of the Sephardim."
Handbook of Palestine, 3rd ed., p. 58.

The Sephardim were first in the field by centuries throughout
the Near and Middle East. Dr. Weizmann's address before the
Basle Congress: unfortunately not of 1918 but of 1931: "One

Early in 1918 Sir Victor Harari Pasha, a well known Jewish figure in Cairo, wrote to me suggesting that I should take his son, then serving in the Camel Corps, on my Staff. By a stroke of genius he enclosed an Italian War stamp, bearing a portrait of Dante with the legend

La domanda onesta
Si dee seguir con l'opera, tacendo.
"To fair request
Silent performance maketh best return."

On such an appeal I would have appointed a crétin. Far from this, Ralph Harari was not only an excellent Finance Officer, but a complete success with Moslem and Christian alike; with all indeed save with an almost ostentatiously-ignoring Zionist Commission. When the Pasha came to visit his son I invited to meet him the leading Moslem dignitaries, and was struck by the immediate cordiality of their relations. They were of the same tradition; they spoke (in every sense) the same language. I am not attempting to praise Harari Pasha at the expense of any member of the Commission when I say that it was the difference between sending the Captain of the Oxford Cricket Eleven to negotiate with a Master of Hounds, and sending Einstein. For weeks after Harari left I was asked by the Mufti and the Mayor what chances there were of the *Basha* revisiting Jerusalem. With all deference to expert opinion, yet speaking as one ceaselessly striving to promote friendships between Arabs and Jews, I cannot but think that more use might and should have been made by the Zionists of the Sephardim.[1]

---

such channel of communication we already possess in our Sephardic communities, with the many ties of language and custom which they have with the Arab peoples among whom they have so long lived."

[1] "The Zionists are completely informed upon every aspect of the problem, save that of Palestine and the Palestinians. They

Some of the Russian leaders seemed rather to glory in having lost that practical and tactful knowledge of men, that imaginative understanding of opponents, which has borne a Disraeli or a Reading so high above the average of humanity. They were in Palestine of right; they were not going to cringe to Sudan-trained officers who treated them like natives (and yet it was as natives that they were returning) and they were inclined to mount "An eye like Mars, to threaten or command"; sometimes both. A Government measure might be Zionistic enough to evoke angry protests from the Arabs: by the other side it was taken as a matter of course. It was a cause of complaint how few of the British knew Hebrew, but when I asked why so few Zionists spoke Arabic the answer was: "We will, when they learn our language."

Dealing with some of these representatives was a sort of intellectual Jiu-Jitsu which I sometimes positively enjoyed, though there were moments when I took secret refuge in Dryden's inspired couplet:

God's pampered people whom, debauch'd with ease,
No king could govern and no God could please.

And I can never forget that for the School of Music, for concerts, for opera, as well as for our Exhibitions of painting and sculpture, I depended for existence upon the Jews. Even here, the painters and sculptors once threatened at the last moment to boycott a *Salon* because for some reason or other I was compelled to admit the public through the smaller external door instead of through the great gate of the Citadel.

Their *Kultur* was exclusively and arrogantly Russian.

---

do not know the languages, nor will they employ the Egyptian Jews who do know them: the consequence is that their frank intentions of policy alarm the present aborigines only less than their reassurances." (Letter to Mark Sykes, 1918.)

Your smatterings of early Latin and Greek, your little
English or other classics that might survive twenty
years marooning out of Europe, were sounding brass
and tinkling cymbals if you had not also Turgenieff,
Gogol and above all Dostoevsky—of whom you were
reminded that no translation conveyed the faintest
reflection. Occasional brain-storms seemed to lift the
curtain and disclose for a moment that deep-seated
intellectual contempt of the Slav for the Briton which,
surviving Czardom, continues to complicate Anglo-
Russian relations. Lord Cromer once wrote that there
was one sort of brain under a hat, quite another sort
under a tarbush. In Jerusalem the thoughts that steamed
from the samovar had small resemblance to those
that issued from the coffee-pot or the decanter: not
worse, not better, but different—as revealed in their
terrifying brilliance at chess, their passion for inter-
minable argument. This impression was not merely
Gentile or anti-Slav prejudice. In the summer of 1918
Levi Bianchini, the Sephardi Captain of an Italian
Dreadnought (and an honour to any navy or nation)
was attached to the Zionist Commission. He confided
to me, with wistful humour, that in Tel Aviv he was
never safe from an unannounced political visitor at
three in the morning until he placed a Marine outside
his house with orders to admit no one out of hours.
He added (and I easily believed) that his action had been
strongly resented.[1] A leading Dutch Sephardi once

---

[1] In August 1920 he was mistaken for a French officer and
murdered in a train by Syrian Arabs, a cruel loss to the cause of
Anglo-Jewish understanding which I recorded in an obituary
letter to the *Palestine Weekly*. "His was the large humanity of a
great and general culture. I remember him on more than one
occasion, when individuals or classes had been giving what the
company in which he found himself considered an unwarrantable
degree of annoyance to the community, repeating with that air
of noble and gentle excuse which so well became him, 'they are
poor people, they are poor people'. I can imagine no anti-Semite,
no Italophobe, no hater-on-principle of Classes or of Govern-

begged me to believe that "what you admire in them is Jewish, and the rest—from beyond !" Hebraists used to complain of the Yiddish and Slavonic "sufferings" of Hebrew pronunciation, causing it to jar in their ears, and sighed for "original" Sephardic. I dare say we were stupid in assuming that these tremendous Russians were like the European Jews we had hitherto known; perhaps they also might have realized sooner that we were not *Chinovniks*; and it took us time to learn one another—time and close association. Meanwhile we regretted that such British, Dutch or (with the exception of the able Dr. Ruppin) German Jews as made their way on to the Commission seemed to count less there than their Russian colleagues, and that there was intense and open soreness at the appointment thereto of a distinguished British officer, Colonel Kisch—of whom it was murmured that he could not be a good Zionist because he played hockey.

There were other bewilderments for British officials mainly concerned with "straight" administration. To some of them it seemed that Jewish[1] political aims occupied too large a proportion of the time and the thoughts of the Administration—that the good administration of the country was no longer the primary end, but that the primary end was becoming a political end. These should logically have resigned, yet some of them were our ablest administrators. There was unease, and mutual criticism within our own ranks. To others the constant leakage of information by telephone and otherwise was disconcerting, though a few of us derived

---

ments who knew him that will not relax something of the tensity of his feeling in a glow of friendliness whenever he remembers the help and the inspiration that were Levi Bianchini."

[1] Mr. Leonard Stein, on the other hand, in his reasonable if necessarily one-sided *Zionism*, while admitting that "The duty of O.E.T.A. was simply to maintain the *Status quo*", adds (on the same page) that "O.E.T.A. only half understood the Balfour Declaration". Presumably that unpopular and unrewarding half which it was nevertheless somebody's business to bear in mind.

a simple pleasure from frustrating these knavish tricks. (I remember snatches of the constantly changing cipher employed between Sir Wyndham Deedes[1] on Mount Scopus and myself by the Damascus Gate. The High Commissioner would be "Queen Elizabeth's husband", the Mufti, "Cantuar", the Latin Patriarch, "He who is above all criticism"; and we doubled in and out of French and Turkish, enriched by tropes and metaphors from the cricket and the hunting field, in our endeavours to baffle the Shūlamīt of the Switchboard.)

If the Administration of Palestine was not altogether beer and skittles for the Gentile official, it must have seemed for some of his British Jewish colleagues little better than one long embarrassment.

On the departure of Major Orme Clark as Legal Adviser the post was filled by his junior, Norman Bentwich, who thus became Attorney-General to the Civil Government. I had known him at Cambridge and in Egypt, and cherished an admiring friendship for an Israelite who, with all his talents, was indeed without guile. Unfortunately Bentwich was not only the son of an original *Hovév Tsiyón*[2] but the author of a book on Zionism which, though written before, appeared after his appointment. As Law Officer it was his duty to draft and to advise the Palestine Governments upon Laws, Proclamations and situations frequently of extreme interest to Jews and Arabs alike, and nothing on earth would convince the Arabs of the impartial purity of his conclusions. "It is not possible," they would answer, "the better Zionist he is, the worse Attorney-General." Some of his British colleagues were inclined to agree that his position was delicate, while he was severely criticized by Zionists for excessive moderation. It is not often that too great love of a country proves a bar from dedicating to it the maturity of one's experience and qualifications, but such was the pathetic

[1] First Chief Secretary to the Civil Administration.
[2] See p. 46.

fate of Bentwich. He refused more than one promotion (including the Chief Justiceship of Cyprus, where he would for good reasons have been welcomed by others besides myself) and finally bowing to the general opinion, abandoned the Palestine Government (but never the Land of Israel) for the Hebrew University. There his first lecture as Professor in the Chair of International Peace was rendered impossible by the behaviour of young Jewish students, to quell which it was found necessary to call in British Police.

Albert Hyamson was a learned and agreeable North-London Orthodox Jew, author of one or two well-written books on Jewish subjects, a figure esteemed and respected not only by his colleagues, but by the Orthodox Jewry of Jerusalem. He had been a British Civil Servant in the General Post Office, and now found himself (via Jewish interests at the Paris Peace Conference) employed as head of the Immigration Department, applying the necessary but complicated regulations for the admission of Jews under the Mandate. These regulations (like those of the Customs for most people) it was for many a point of honour as well as a pleasure to defeat; and the families of temporary brothers and sisters, the relays of spinster wives and married fiancées all destined for the same husband, the arrivals on a three-months' permit who never become departures, severely test the vigilance of the Controller. Hyamson accepted or rejected applications with the conscientiousness traditional in the British Civil Service, and in consequence soon became one of the most unpopular figures in pan-Zionism; which has created of him the brazen image of a Jack-in-office, sadistically thrusting back the persecuted immigrant for the sake of a misprint in his passport—an image that the scores of thousands of Jews admitted through his Department have not yet availed to demolish.

My observations on some of the difficulties of the Administrator, especially with East European Zionists, are written in no less good faith than is the rest of my book, yet I feel that I may not have allowed for the sensitiveness of two thousand years' ill-treatment. I have mentioned the admirable entertainment[1] given by the 60th Division within two months of the taking of Jerusalem. To avoid all risk of offence, I had checked the programme myself. On the second evening a performer was taken ill at the last moment, and a surprise number substituted. He proved (without intentional offence) to be a caricature of the "ol' clo'" music-hall Jew, and I could have wished him anything (and anywhere) else in the world, especially when two or three Jews rose and walked out of the house. At the time I thought their sensibility was exaggerated, and I continued to think so until the autumn of 1935, when after a fortnight in a friendly and courteous Venice, I stayed a few days in Paris, and was taken to the *Théâtre de Dix Heures*. There, mingled with several witty and delightful recitations, I found myself listening consecutively to three scurrilous and ignoble attacks upon the motives and honour of England. In the misery of my impotent indignation I suddenly realized, and knew I could never forget, something of what these Jews had felt.

I have suggested that no monopoly of error can be ascribed to any one of the three interested parties of Palestine, and I have attempted to indicate one or two respects in which the British Government, as well as the Zionist Executive, might conceivably have been better advised.

People who consider themselves martyrs are not on that account necessarily saints. Some of the Arabs in their bewilderment and indignation more than repaid the injustices they felt they were suffering from British as well as Jews. It was not long before Arab Nationalism, despairing of other weapons, had recourse to fanaticism and reaction, notably after the death of the old Mufti,

[1] v. *Orientations*, p. 341.

Kāmel al-Husseini; and the Government was (as happens sometimes in private life) most bitterly vilified by those who had best reason to be grateful. I have come upon my Minute on a report of the Chief Secretary's interview with a notorious agitator:

"Interesting as showing in a very mild version the lines on which the Shaikh perorates when assured of no cold light of fact upon his invective. Every statement is either an *expressio* or a *suggestio falsi*. No Arab Nationalist is 'dogged because of his Nationalism with spies' (? Secret Agents), who are reserved in Palestine, as in other countries under British rule (but in no independent Oriental country), for persons whose actions are likely to bring about a breach of the peace. The Government has dealt with particular leniency with the Shaikh himself, as he is well aware; and has, so far from attempting to work against the Supreme Moslem Council, refused to listen officially to much not unjustified criticism against a worthy if inexperienced body which it has itself created and consistently supported."

The British Administration, Military and Civil, had from the first extended to Arab Moslems a sympathetic encouragement they had never received from the Moslem Turks. The Northern façade of the Dome of the Rock[1] was saved by no Arab initiative, but by British application for a British architect; and when funds were needed to extend the repairs to the Mosque of al-Aqsa (after Mecca and Medina the most sacred shrine in Islam) the leaders of Arab agitation were not only permitted, but encouraged and assisted by the generous liberalism of the High Commissioner to make collections throughout the Moslem world. (His honourable confidence was justified.) Under British rule every piastre of the Moslem religious endowments was now used exclusively for Moslem purposes in Palestine,

[1] Known to tourists as the Mosque of Omar.

instead of being largely diverted to Constantinople; and certain wealthy endowments, sequestered by the Porte eighty years before, were returned to the Waqf authority. Apart from other direct benefactions, there can be no doubt whatever that all the material and some of the intellectual amenities of life were multiplied by the stimulus of Jewish resources fostered under a British Administration. It might have been supposed that a Chamber of Commerce would be unobnoxious to religious sectarianism, even in Jerusalem; yet its inception was for a while suspended because Moslems, though constantly proclaiming their identity of interest with their Christian brethren, were holding out for larger representation.

This unhappy attitude was accentuated by a tendency frequently observable in peoples (and in persons) recently liberated from long and tyrannical oppression. Nothing, as the British found in Egypt of the 'eighties, could be more immediately delightful than to succeed an Ottoman Turkish regime. For the first few weeks all is joy, hope and passionate gratitude. But it is not long before the late victims begin to discover that British prosperity is less immediate than they had hoped, and that meanwhile the irksome payment of taxes or compliance with new-fangled sanitary regulations can no longer be evaded by influence or bakshish. "By Allah!" things were better under the Othmanli.[1] (Moses himself went through this on the frequent occasions when the whole congregation murmured against him.) They also discover that under the mild impersonal British rule lapses from manners (hitherto ruinous) pass unnoticed, anyhow unpunished: and some will soon venture upon presumptions and rudenesses they would never have attempted under their former masters.

[1] Their extremists overreached or stultified themselves when, for instance, the Mufti declared to the Royal Commission: "Under the Ottoman Constitution the Arabs enjoyed all rights and privileges political and otherwise, on an equal basis with the Turks"!

As is said in the Egyptian proverb: "They fear, but
do not respect." The temptation grows to attitudinize
before their public, to brave dangers of floggings and
hangings which they well know they will never be called
upon to endure. Sir Eldon Gorst used to say that his
prestige in Egypt would be immeasurably enhanced if
only he could commit once a year one act of glaring
illegality, the bazaars arguing: "if the Ruler must
obey the Law like me, how is he my Superior?" The
French Administration in Syria had frequent and double
tastes of these impertinences, when Damascus cried:
"Give us all the Zionists in the world, if only under
British rule", while Jerusalem answered: "Give us
even French exploitation, provided it be without
Zionism."

In a word, what with the feasts, the fasts, and the
anniversaries, the impassioned conferences and con-
gresses with the resulting journalistic diatribes; what
with the protests, the boycottings, the shuttings of
shops, the stupid provocations and the disgusting
retaliations, there were those among us who would
cry, with Mercutio, "A plague on both your houses!"
and would sigh for the appointment of some "crusted"
African or West Indian Colonial Governor, who would
"knock their heads together", or "give them something to cry for".

Here then were two parties each with a strong case
to plead, yet, each being his own lawyer, having but
too often (as the saying is) a fool for his client. The
Arab patriot adjuring his hearers not to allow one foot
of the sacred soil conquered by their forefathers to pass
into the clutch of the obscene invader, might sometimes be himself a land-broker, only too anxious to sell
his own and his friends' property to buyers of any land
and of all nationalities. Zion could muster many able
but some irritatingly disingenuous pens, arguing for
instance that the French troubles in Syria proved that

D

ours were not due to Zionism, and would have befallen us under any dispensation.[1]

The earliest recognition I received in Europe of the realities of the British officer's position in Palestine was from the lips of Mr. Lloyd George. I had first met him during the Peace Conference, and he was good enough to invite me to breakfast with him alone at 10 Downing Street. Greeting me sternly, he remarked that complaints of me were reaching him from Jews and Arabs alike. I answered that this was all too probable, imagining for a moment from his tone that he was leading up to my resignation. "Well," he said as we sat down, "If either one side stops complaining—you'll be dismissed." A principle which should hearten All Ranks in the Palestine Service for some decades to come.

IV

Car l'impossible, voilà notre tache. NIETZSCHE.

Such then were the phases of the situation and the sentiments of those therewith concerned during the eight years from 1918 to 1925.

After the crowded quinquennium of Sir Herbert Samuel, something of a halt was called in construction. For three years Lord Plumer sat on Mount Scopus. Under the shadow of that great name Palestine knew so

---

[1] Zionism had at least united (for the first time in history) Arab Moslems and Christians, who now opposed a single front to the Mandatory. During a crisis between the Moslems and Christians of Syria this dialogue appeared in the Damascus newspaper *al-Maarad*:
Christ. "What is the way, O Muhammad, to set our two nations, Syria and Lebanon, in unison?"
Muhammad. "Ask Moses to send them a party of his men."
It is true that since France assumed the Syrian Mandate in 1920 six High Commissioners had until 1939 failed to bring peace to Syria, or to prevent the thirteen national revolutions that have taken place.

perfect a peace that the Government denuded it of all its defences—as the succeeding competent but unfortunate Administration found to their cost in the ghastly summer of 1929. The bitterness surviving that tragedy was still evident in 1931, when I observed an almost complete social cleavage between the British and the Jewish communities. Since then Palestine had gone so rapidly ahead, in wealth as well as in population, that by the spring of 1936 I felt justified, despite one or two anxious letters from Arabs and Jews, in writing: "The present High Commissioner has succeeded in winning the confidence of the Jews to a degree unattained by any of his predecessors, and has had the good fortune (and the courage) to have his term extended for a further period of five years. He has under him, permanently stationed, a repressive force such as no other High Commissioner has wielded, so that, whatever other problems may assail him, he is at least free from that haunting obsession—the breakdown of Public Security. . . ." Prophecy is indeed the most gratuitous of human errors.

If this chapter has contained more of British lack of policy and of the difficulties of practical Zionism than of Arab errors and crimes (the word cannot be avoided), the reason is in part that Zion and England stand responsible as creators of the situation.[1] As wielders of all the resources of modern civilization, it was for them to set a pace which native Palestine could follow. As springing from the New Testament as well as from the Old, and from the gracious humanism of the ancient world, it was theirs to call a tune with which the rhythms of simpler peoples might without violence be moulded

[1] "We insisted upon having the mandate for Palestine assigned to us. We also virtually dictated the terms upon which the Council of the League endorsed the action of the Principal Allied Powers, and made itself responsible for supervising our mandatory administration." *Economist*, March 1936.

into counter-point. The cumulative result of their combined failure in London and in Palestine was an explosion of feeling so momentous that the greatest Power in the world, after near twenty years' experiment and experience, required, in full peace time, an Army Corps and all the panoply of war to control the "liberated" civil population; and the Arabs are able to boast that in calling off a guerilla warfare maintained for six months, they yielded neither to British arms nor to the economic necessity of salving their orange crop, but to the advice of an Arab Dreikaiserbund of Iraq-Saūdi-Arabia and Transjordan, and have thus established an institution and a precedent no less unpalatable to Britain than to Zion.

I suppose it was the mutual reaction of accelerated Jewish immigration and a period of exhilarating prosperity and intensive construction which seemed to justify the argument that, if with 1,000 immigrants prosperity appears to increase 100 per cent., then with 10,000 it will increase 1,000 per cent., with 100,000 10,000 per cent.; that if there is at a given moment economic absorptive capacity for greatly increased immigration, the increase should forthwith be authorized; and that, as the Arabs complain anyhow, a few score extra thousands make no particular difference. At all events the curve of authorized entry, and with it unauthorized, grew spectacularly steeper after 1932; the authorized reaching 31,000 and 42,000 for the next two years, and culminating in the record figure of 61,849 for 1935, to say nothing of the ten thousand clandestine but undeniable additions. At this point it was apparently felt that something must be done to placate the "non-Jewish" population;[1] and the establishment of the Legislative Council (promised in the White Paper of 1930) on a basis of numerically proportionate repre-

[1] This thesis does not commend itself to Lord Melchett. *Thy Neighbour*, vide pp. 226-7.

sentation was put forward by the High Commissioner in Council; approved by the Secretary of State for the Colonies; announced by the High Commissioner in December 1935; and published to the world. The proposal was welcomed by the Arabs as a whole, especially by the more intelligent who stand to gain by an increase of civilization, though a few hesitated lest its acceptance should involve or imply their acceptance of the Mandate. It was immediately boycotted by the Jews. Dr. Weizmann hurried back from Palestine, just in time for the Commons Debate. "The heavy brigades of Press, platform and Parliament", I wrote, "are being wheeled into action against the proposal for a Legislative Council, though this is implicit in the Mandate and explicitly promised to the people as well as to the League of Nations, besides being recommended by a High Commissioner whom the Jews have good cause to trust. There is much to be said against the establishment of representative legislatures in unsuitable Mediterranean countries, as successive High Commissioners and Governors of Cyprus and Malta have found to their cost. But this is not the chief or original objection of the Zionists, who attack the project because the Jews are to be allotted seats in proportion to their actual population; going so far as to postulate that there should be no sort of constitution until Jews are in parity or a majority and so able to safeguard the key provisions of the Mandate—and this though all reference to the National Home, Immigration and kindred subjects is already ruled rigorously out of order in the debates of the Council. Yet if ever a people seem to deserve at least the opportunity of official public utterance, it is the Arabs of Palestine. The National Government happily for its own good name, resisted this last clamour, whose only effect was to convince the Arabs, hitherto hesitant for fear of appearing to accept the Mandate, that there must be something to their

advantage in a project so bitterly denounced by the
Jews. (In March 1923, when the Legislative Council
was first proposed and was boycotted by the Arabs, the
Jewish Press was indignant at the 'weakness' of the
Government and asked: 'Now that elections have been
ordered by an Order-in-Council and it was proclaimed
that anyone interfering with the elections would be
prosecuted, why was this not carried out? Why was
not the poisonous agitation stopped ?') "

In the subsequent debate in both Houses, the Arab
case may be said, without exaggeration, to have gone by
default. A Zionist listener in the Gallery of the Commons
might have been edified by hearing speech after speech
showing intimate knowledge even of the details of the
Zionist side, and dismissing, as semi-comic, the "*donums,
eddans*—acres or whatever they call them" of the Arabs.
One voice interjected: "Are there not Arab capitalists ?"
Mr. Winston Churchill, Public Orator of the British
Empire, adroitly shifting his ground to the German
treatment of Jews, shouted aloud, "Vile tyranny !"
and shook his fist at the ceiling. Not a soul could dis-
agree with him; yet the Germans admitted among the
record entry of 61,849 amounted to less than 16 per cent.
Mr. J. H. Thomas took shelter behind his Geneva
obligations and, although the Government escaped
defeat by its own supporters, the world knew that the
Palestine Legislative Council was adjourned *sine die*
before it had ever been opened. No doubt all these
speakers were logically right, and perhaps Parliament
should have been spontaneously consulted before the
taking of so momentous a decision; yet the immediate
adoption of the Council might have proved cheaper,
and could not have proved dearer, in treasure, prestige
and blood—British as well as Jewish and Arab—than
its rejection. On the principle of "no hope can have no
fear" the Arabs, now desperate, embarked upon a
"peaceful strike" which inevitably degenerated into the

situation in which Great Britain found herself contemplated by the ironic amusement of the Nations.
Moderate Arab leaders, unencouraged by any prospect
of association with the Government of their country,
and so with no motive for assisting it, were reluctantly
compelled to stand in with extremists. Arab violence,
resulting largely from the manner of the Commons'
and still more of the Lords' rejection of the Legislative
Council, was now claimed by the Zionists as the immediate justification thereof. Arms for the insurgents,
as well as money, poured in from neighbouring countries,
perhaps also from a more distant Power. It was, therefore, still possible though highly disingenuous to argue
that the insurrection was not spontaneous, but engineered
from abroad. The appointment of a Royal Commission[1]
failed to stop what was becoming a small war; though it
succeeded in alarming the Zionists, who feared that its
recommendations could tend, however slightly, in
but one direction.[2] Both they and other thinking people
revolted at the suggestion of yielding to violence—a
Danegeld to which especially in the East there is no
limit; some seeming to forget that this general violence
had followed, and was in great part the result of, five
peaceful and unsuccessful delegations to Whitehall and
six special but often unimplemented Commissions to
Palestine. It cannot be questioned that violence on
this occasion succeeded to the extent of bringing about
the appointment of the Royal Commission, and in the
increased interest and numbers of the "Arab" committee in the House of Commons. All parties in England
were agreed that violence must unquestionably and
unconditionally cease or be made to cease: and that

[1] Advocated by *The Times* in a leading article entitled *Political
Zionism* on 11 April 1922.
[2] *Palestine* ingenuously supported Lord Lytton's previous proposal for a Royal Commission to examine (and to modify or
prevent) the Legislative Council, as being "intelligible". "But
. . . a Commission of this kind . . . alarming. . . ."

the Royal Commission should then lose no time in proceeding to Palestine.[1] Whatever its conclusions, or whatever the degree of their acceptance by the Government and the Legislature may be, there are meanwhile certain considerations bearing upon both sides of the problem which, judging by recent declarations, appear even now to be but imperfectly appreciated. The Arabs base their opposition to the terms of the Mandate upon the following arguments:

(*a*) It is contrary to their natural right to their country.

(*b*) It is contrary to British and Allied pledges given to the Arabs.

(*c*) It violates the general principles of the "Mandate" as set forth in Article 22 of the Covenant of the League.

(*d*) It is self-contradictory.

(*e*) It menaces and endangers their existence, present and future, and stands as an unsurmountable obstacle in the path of their national aspirations and political goal.

They will be well advised to cut out (*a*) and (*b*), and to concentrate upon the remainder, of which the Royal Commission is empowered to examine the force. With regard to (*b*), Palestine was excluded from the promises made to Arabs before those British operations which gave freedom to so large a proportion of the Arab peoples. The claim, though still credited by many, has been so often disproved that it is no longer a bargaining asset. As for (*a*), I cannot do better than quote the sober words of Lord Milner: "If the Arabs go to the length of claiming Palestine as one of their countries in the same sense as Mesopotamia or Arabia proper is an Arab country, then I think they are flying in the face of facts, of all history, of all tradition, and of associations

---

[1] The reader is here referred to the first two sentences of the Postscript, p. 121, to which I have added a still briefer P.P.S. bringing the narrative up to the Spring of 1940.

of the most important character—I had almost said, the most sacred character. Palestine can never be regarded as a country on the same footing as the other Arab countries. You cannot ignore all history and tradition in the matter. You cannot ignore the fact that this is the cradle of two of the great religions of the world. It is a sacred land to the Arabs, but it is also a sacred land to the Jew and to the Christian." The sooner, therefore, that they abandon these two theses, and concentrate upon possibly remediable grievances, the sooner are they likely to obtain a measure of satisfaction. Whatever measure they do obtain they should strive by peaceful and lawful endeavour to maintain or even to improve, remembering that any subsequent resort to violence could not fail to lose them the degree of sympathy they have recently acquired, and so to be more sharply and severely repressed. They must learn, above all, that it is precisely persons sufficiently balanced and humane to realize that there is an Arab side to Zionism who will be most profoundly revolted and alienated by such specimens of Arabian chivalry as the shooting of a Jewish scholar at his desk, of a hospital nurse on the steps of her hospital and the bombing of a baby's perambulator. The Turkish proverb " *Baluq bashdan kokar*"—"The fish goes rotten from the head" —applies here; and "Leaders" who not only fail to prevent but refuse to denounce this filthiness forfeit all claim to honourable consideration, and might well be made to answer personally for the crimes their attitude has undoubtedly encouraged. Their behaviour, and that of their followers, loses yet further when contrasted with that of the Jews,[1] whose austere self-discipline under such outrages and the destruction for many of their life-work has won them the admiration of the civilized world. If the Arabs are reasonably successful in removing the "menace to their existence, present and

[1] But see P.P.S., p. 121.

future" cited in (e), they might find themselves in a stronger position by accepting the Mandate—perhaps under some further solemn instrument, ratified by the Mandatory and the League, and possibly endorsed by any Powers specially interested. Their acceptance would pave the way to extensions of administrative and legislative autonomy which I shall indicate later, but which could not be contemplated so long as they stood out. The policy I have advocated requires a facing of facts which, as often in life, entails certain undeniable but in my opinion inevitable renunciations, only tolerable upon the receipt of immediate and tangible advantage.

Zionism provides a close parallel to Arab argument (b) in the "Agreement" of 3 January 1919 between the Amir Faisal and Dr. Weizmann, frequently claimed as "the specific acceptance of the National Home Policy". As the recognized champion of the Arab cause, Faisal was within his rights in excluding[1] from his claims a section of the Arab world for the supposed benefit of the whole; but by so doing he debarred himself from further dealing with that section. Similarly the note by Faisal translated for Dr. Weizmann by Lawrence and reproduced in *The Times* of 10 June 1936 is of interest as evidence of co-operation between two outstanding personalities, and as a holograph specimen of Lawrence's forceful handwriting; but since neither Faisal nor Lawrence was empowered or any longer competent to represent the Arabs of Palestine, it is not relevant.[2]

Zionists high and low in the Press and on the platform still appear bewildered at the continual opposition and

[1] "On account of its universal character I shall leave Palestine on one side for the mutual consideration of all parties interested; with this exception, I ask for the independence of the Arabic areas enumerated in the Memorandum."

[2] Yet, late in 1936: "there can be no evasion of the plain terms of the agreement entered into on 3 January 1919 between the Amir Faisal on behalf of the Arab Kingdom of the Hejaz and Dr. Weizmann . . ." *Thy Neighbour.*

"obstinacy" of the Arabs. "Arab birth-rates have gone up: Arab death and infant mortality rates have gone down. Out of the quarter of a million Public Health Vote nine-tenths is devoted to Arabs. The Arab standard of life has risen beyond all expectation. Arabs are making money . . .": Yet still . . . ! Arab objections "therefore cannot be economic: they must be 'political'." Zionists will not yet admit to themselves, certainly not to the world, that the Palestine Arab[1] has for hundreds of years considered Palestine, a country no larger than Wales, as his home; and that he does not consider that there is, within those limits, room for another home, to be stocked "as of right" from a reserve of sixteen million people. From the Jewish point of view Zionism, involving many sacrifices, is an idealistic movement. For the inhabitant of Palestine it is entirely materialistic, nationalistic, acquisitive, and non-religious. The injunction, oft repeated, to Arabs "to work with Jews to develop their common country" is a mere irritation, for it is only their common country by virtue of a bond which those most affected there have not yet accepted. The Zionist slogan so reasonable-sounding in England, "neither to dominate nor to be dominated", has, if it means anything like numerical equality[2]—and what else can it mean ?—a frosty sound in the ears of a poorer, backward occupant. And when a British journalist

[1] The position was ably stated in the above-quoted leading article in *The Times* on 11 April 1922.

[2] " . . . political majority of the Jews. There is nothing in the Mandate to prevent this. . . . But we have claimed political parity as a right—let us give it as a right to the Arabs." *Thy Neighbour*, p. 251.

"We say to the Arabs, taking full responsibility for our words; to-day we are in a minority; to-morrow we may be the majority; to-day you are the majority, to-morrow you may be a minority. Whatever may happen in Palestine, we do not want to dominate or be dominated. We want to be there as equals. We have the greatest respect for your language, your religion, your holy places. But we, on the other hand, ask you to respect our religion, language, our labour, and our lives !" Dr. Weizmann in an address at Antwerp. *The New Judaea*, October 1936, p. 5.

of repute writes[1] (in a widely reproduced article):
"Politically I believe it would be wise to build the
National Home as rapidly as possible, even by shock
tactics. So long as the Jewish minority grows slowly,
year by year, the Arabs will fight against destiny. But
when instead of the present 28 per cent, the Jewish
population amounts to a clear 50 or 40 per cent, they
will bow to accomplished facts. When the Jews are
strong enough to defend themselves, there will be no
more talk about driving them into the sea. The German
problem strengthens this argument for haste"—is he
not inviting the Arabs to take a leaf out of his own
book? The plain truth which, twenty years after the
Balfour Declaration, must be faced is, that the Arabs of
Palestine rejected it from the first and will never accept
it unless something is done to assure them their economic,
territorial and national survival. In this they are only
ranging themselves with other and far larger countries
or nations, including those of the British Empire, which
have long since ceased to tolerate foreign large-scale
immigration, particularly from eastern Europe. To
evoke or account for such universal sentiments neither
"*Effendis*"[2] nor "foreign gold" are necessary: though
it is not unnatural that Arab leaders should lead, nor
that they should clutch at support from whatever quarter.
With the dropping of the bogey of the politically as
well as economically exploiting *Effendi*, propaganda
might be simultaneously lightened by that of the sinister
British official, whether hampering the zeal of the High
Commissioner in Palestine or in the Colonial Office
breathing evil counsels into the ear of the well-disposed
but all too dependent Secretary of State.[3] Entrants into

---

[1] H. N. Brailsford in *The Baltimore Sun*.

[2] "Nevertheless the Palestinian Jews . . . recognize that the
peasant Arabs have been made the tool of Sectional and partizan
interests." *Thy Neighbour*, pp. 248-9.

[3] Even in 1937 the legend is kept alive (before the Royal Commission) by Colonel Wedgwood: "The permanent officials regarded

the Palestine arena might well bear in mind the placard said to be displayed in Japanese restaurants: "Visitors bring their own manners." Is it not conceivable that officers on the spot, grappling year after year with the difficulties of reconciling both sides of the Mandate, may have as just an appreciation thereof as persons, often in another continent or hemisphere, concerned solely with the advancement of their own cause?[1]

There can be no question of surrendering the Mandate; of stopping immigration; or of continuing it on the recent intensive scale. What the basis of the scale should be, the Royal Commission may possibly indicate. But it can hardly attain for many years the hitherto accepted principle of 100 per cent entry according to the economic absorptive capacity[2] of Palestine at the moment of authorization. To absorb is not always to digest. There are reasons other than "political" for reduction. Early in 1936 the question of a subsidy to orange-growers was being raised by sections of the citrus industry, which already found it difficult to market nine and a half million boxes and trembled at the thought of placing the twenty to twenty-five million boxes anticipated in ten years time. And in general, the aftermath of a construction period, however brilliant, is a serious problem for the constructing trades and professions.[3] The

Palestine as their enemy", he said. "They had in Palestine an Administration of 'crypto-Fascist officials', whose objections to Parliament had taken the place of objections to the Jews. There is no change except by a complete reform of the Administration in Palestine."

[1] Already in 1922 Philip Graves, then Special Correspondent for *The Times* in Palestine, records the Zionist practice of "ascribing their difficulties to the perversity of the Arabs, the intrigues of the Catholics", above all to the "lack of sympathy" or "hostility" of British officials.

[2] "'The economic absorptive capacity of the country," was a partially irrelevant and thoroughly misleading phrase.'" *Survey of British Commonwealth Affairs*, 1918–36.

[3] As the Government of Northern Rhodesia found to their cost with hundreds of stranded and unemployable artisans on their hands when the price of copper fell.

impartial arbitrator could hardly fail to be interested by Dr. Weizmann's estimate[1] that Palestine could within the next fifty years support between fifty and sixty thousand more Jewish families, with an additional 100,000 agricultural Arabs, on the water supply now existing or soon procurable: and considerably more of both if that supply could be increased. It seems further possible that a Legislative Council on something near the lines of that which was frozen out in 1936, might be reintroduced; and that the Zionists and associated forces would not repeat their mistake by opposing it again. As Mr. Amery has written: "To go on refusing representative Government as long as the Jews are in a minority is an almost impossible policy."

The extreme and logical anti-Zionists (or pro-Arabs— they cannot be differentiated, though some would like to have it both ways) are for what they call a "clean sweep", meaning the abolition of the Mandate; apparently imagining that Palestine would nevertheless remain under British control, at all events proposing no alternative solution. Their opinions would command more respect if they organized themselves into some constituted public body prepared to devote time, brains and cash to the cause of an Arab as the Zionist has to a Jewish Palestine. Even so, they would shake not the Mandate but the Mandatory, Great Britain, whose place more than one Great Power would be only too happy (though certainly not more competent) to occupy. The Mandate, as I have said, cannot be shaken, for it is the united voice of fifty-two peoples speaking through the League of Nations, which for all its defects is the

[1] Address delivered to the Royal Central Asian Society, 26 May 1936. The above figures are not recorded in the official summary of the proceedings. The census of 1931 estimated that, if present trends were continued, the population of Palestine would double itself in twenty years, the Moslem population in twenty-five years and the Jewish population in nine years. The Jewish population in 1931 was 17 per cent. of the total population of Palestine: in 1935 27 per cent.

nearest approach to a world conscience hitherto evolved
by humanity. No man (as Aristotle wrote), deliberates
about that which cannot be otherwise. The Mandate
stands; but if the facts I have endeavoured to record
have any significance, they may point to the possibility,
without heroic measures (which no one has yet been able
to suggest), of easing its application.

A solution that has been discussed, and of which the
logical reasons and advantages have of late been in-
geniously elaborated, is that of Cantonization, Partition
or Division, whereby the Jews in the Maritime Plains
and the Arabs in the Hill Country would form two more
or less self-governing communities or cantons, with
certain matters reserved, and a general supervision
exercised by a High Commissioner in a neutralized
and directly administered Jerusalem. The theory,
though apparently unassailable when taken point by
point, seems unlikely of adoption; as contravening the
spirit of the Mandate, as tending to erect two potentially
hostile camps within a very small area and—perhaps the
strongest objection—as being wholly unacceptable to
the feelings and aspirations of the parties concerned.
Nevertheless, Cantonization shines through the fog of
mutual criticism and abuse as an attempt to deal con-
structively with a rarely difficult problem: and economic
or territorial, as apart from political or administrative
cantonization may yet have to be considered. I can
pretend to no such drastic remedy. Indeed, some of
the following observations with the inferences there-
from may be criticized as unimportant or inessential—
as very small beer. If so, I would remind these critics
of their constant employment of the useful term
imponderabilia. The smaller and the more obvious,
the easier considered; as was proved by Naaman, the
Captain of the Host.

One would have supposed for instance that some at
least of the Jewish youth of both sexes would be given

so intensive a knowledge of the sister language, Arabic, that they might not only converse with Arabs as friends and read the Arab Press of their own and neighbouring countries, but also make some local contribution to the mediaeval and modern history of Palestine (the only period interesting to Arabs), or to comparative Semitics. I remember taking the Chair for a great Jewish orientalist when he lectured on Arabic Literature. The room was crowded with Arab extremists hushed in reverent admiration; and for one hour at least there were three score anti-Zionists the less in Jerusalem. Again, I thought a God-intended opportunity was missed over the Kadoorie Bequest. Kadoorie was a rich Shanghai Jew who left some £100,000 to the cause of Education in Palestine. The Government proposed that there should be one college on public school lines for both races, with separate provision for each religion and language. The Arabs made no demur, but the Jews were utterly uncompromising for two separate institutions; and they had their way, excluding even the alternative of a joint School of Agriculture, since they insisted on Hebrew as the language of instruction throughout. The Arabs raised no objection to either proposal, even if English were to be used. The Jews refused partly on the ground that they had not waited two thousand years to become standard public school types. That objection might have been met (though there are worse Englishmen, and Jews, than our Jews from the public schools), and the college modified accordingly; but when some of us reflected upon the generous sympathies and friendships so easy to form at school, so difficult in after-life, we wondered whether the risk of a little British conventionality might not have been worth taking. It is no object of the Mandatory, and far from the spirit of the Mandate, to turn Palestinians of any creed (even if it were possible) into Britons, though all enjoy the coveted privilege of a British passport.

A public service would be rendered to Palestine if one or two well-known Jewish—particularly British Jewish—families of independent means, with no decoration to gain or promotion to miss, would build houses in the neighbourhood of Jerusalem and reside there for some months in the year. Society under Mandated or Crown Colony Government is apt to degenerate into a cross between a Garrison Town and a Cathedral City, and to be overwhelmed by the official element. I know something of the difficulty of entertaining mixed assemblies in Jerusalem, and though I did my best with the means I had, I was conscious that it might have been better done on ground unconnected with politics or administration.

Zionists have repeatedly declared that they do not desire to build up the National Home to the detriment of the Arabs of Palestine. It is therefore all the more unfortunate that the Arabs should have seen almost every step taken by His Majesty's Government to reassure them, vehemently and sometimes successfully assailed. In 1929, Sir John Hope Simpson, an impartial expert in Land Settlement,[1] was appointed from the League of Nations in order to ascertain the area available for agriculture and immigration. His report submitted in 1931 let loose a tempest of Zionist indignation, effective, it must be allowed, in that the Government, though apparently accepting his recommendations, has wholly failed to carry them out. The statement of Government policy (based on the above Report and that of the Shaw Commission) embodied in the White Paper of 1930, which served to allay certain Arab apprehensions, was howled down all over the Jewish world. It may have been unfortunately worded. At all events the British Government disavowed its own Department

[1] Of such eminence that after a similar mission to Greece he was subsequently sent by the League for the same purpose to China.

and recanted; with a re-explanation from the Prime Minister. A triumph indeed for Dr. Weizmann (and not his first in Downing Street) but, in its result of confirming the worst fears of the Arabs, a Pyrrhic victory. Again, a proposal based on Lord Kitchener's Five Feddan Law in Egypt, to protect the small holder, enjoys a significantly poor Hebrew Press. Even if this law were less of a protection to the *Fellah* than the Administration anticipates, criticism of its ineffectiveness would have come more convincingly from the Arab side.

The Arabs, though handicapped in many respects, have certain undeniable compensations. They are, the Jews have to become, acclimatized. They still hold a large proportion of the land which, if they will but take advantage of the training available, should provide for their natural and probable increase of population. They must remember that for available world acreage 1936 is, in their own phrase, *Akhr al-Zaman*—"the end of time"; that the day is past for picturesque feudalism, and that if they do not make the best of their own soil, others will. They should look to it—a Legislative Council would help them in this also—that every possible piastre of the Waqf income is spent upon a vocational education based on the best advice they can procure, and they should demand something more than a published accounting audit to make sure their wishes are obeyed. They should endeavour—but this is asking a hard thing—to leave their foolish Husseini-Nashāshībi feuds to join the Montagus and Capulets and the Middle Ages. The Mandate once accepted, there should be no further objection to the scheme wherewith I wearied the Colonial Office from Cyprus and in London for six long years; to wit the higher promotion within the territory,[1] or the transfer to service in other Mandated

[1] With the object of finally assuring both Maréchal Lyautey's ideal of "*non pas un pouvoir de façade, mais une part effective dans l'Administration et une véritable autorité pour la garantie de leurs coutumes et de leurs libertés*".

Territories or suitable Crown Colonies, of exceptionally qualified local public servants, both Arab and Jew. I shall recur to this topic, only remarking now that I know more than one Palestinian who could have served elsewhere with distinction as well as with stimulus and encouragement to the Palestine Service. Some years ago I was asked by a High Commissioner designate whether I had any recommendation to propose. I suggested the nomination of two Arabs and a Jew to the Executive Council. The system worked excellently in Cyprus, with two Greeks and one Turk, who rendered valuable advice, whose sense of responsibility was greatly increased, and who to the best of my knowledge never proved unworthy of the confidence reposed in them. Both of these developments would diminish the temptation of the local authority to support, for the sake of peace and a quiet life, the extremist rather than the potential co-operator in the work of the Government. Such distinguished Palestinians should be personally and worthily received in London by the Secretary of State.

Any finding of the Royal Commission—from the establishment of a Jewish State to the repudiation of the Balfour Declaration—must entail a double disillusion;[1] for the unquestionable maintenance of the

[1] The statesmanlike decision of the Secretary of State not to suspend but to limit immigration pending results from the Royal Commission was thus reported in *Palestine*, 11 November 1936: "The Colonial Secretary's statement in the House of Commons concerning the limitation of immigration has made a bad impression on the Arabs. The Arabs hoped and perhaps believed that immigration would be entirely suspended during the sittings of the Royal Commission. This was reported to the leaders in Jerusalem by Mr. Emile Ghory, the representative of the Arab Higher Committee in London. The decision not to suspend Jewish immigration, but to grant a labour schedule, however small, has created profound disappointment among the Arab leaders.

The Executive of the Jewish Agency has issued a statement: 'The Executive of the Jewish Agency cannot but express its regret

Mandate would be the end of any national hope still cherished by the Palestinian Arabs, while the Jews could hardly fail to be mortified by any retarding of Immigration, as well as apprehensive of the effect of any Legislative Council. What is of paramount importance for the future of Palestine is that such recommendations of the Commission as may be adopted by the British Government and approved by the League of Nations should be fully, immediately, and lastingly implemented and, above all, subject to no further exposition or apology. Neither the Jews nor the Arabs conquered Palestine from the Turks, but the British—as may be tragically proved by a visit to any of the great War Cemeteries there. British arms must continue to hold the ring against all local or foreign menace. The "need to rule", so often urged upon the Palestine authorities, exists elsewhere than on the Palestine front. Already in June 1921 I wrote:

"The King's birthday passed without untoward event save that the High Commissioner's statement created alarm and despondency throughout Zionist camps, and gave, because of its indefiniteness, coldish comfort to the Arabs, who have received far too many reassurances, but expect nothing less than definite Goods of some sort or other."

How many statements have been issued since then, and what have they profited? Such topics can be treated more naturally and less controversially in an Annual Report, prepared like those of Lord Cromer (which used to be an event in London and in Europe as well as in Egypt), and not on the stereotyped Crown Colony model, further neutralized to conform with the *questionnaires*

---

at the extreme smallness of the present schedule, which it considers inadequate to satisfy even the most urgent requirements of economic development.'"

of Geneva. It is by a firm and undeviating practice
(the word policy is somewhat blown upon in the
promised, half-promised, twice-promised Land), rather
than by explanation and counter-explanation, assurance
and reassurance, or White Papers however "satis-
factorily" drafted, that the Mandatory will maintain
confidence—unshaken, unseduced, unterrified. Zionists
might also refrain from giving the impression that they
are only prepared to support the British Representative
so long as he conforms exactly with their desires. On
the other hand, there is both in official Palestine and at
home an unfair tendency to put all the blame upon the
Jews for the policy, incidents and situations which have
complicated the progress of Mandated Palestine. Though
individual Zionists have sometimes shown themselves
more provocative to Arabs than appreciative of British
endeavour, Zionism is right to put a plenary construction
on the Mandate; and it is the British themselves who
are exclusively responsible for any original defects of
policy, and who have more than once had only themselves to thank for the results of ill-considered yieldings
to the various and powerful influences of the Zionist
Organization.[1] Whenever, after full consideration,
His Majesty's Government has held firm, no party has
ultimately been the loser. When for instance the first
issue of Palestine stamps was being designed, strong
pressure was exerted upon the authorities to render
Palestine, in the Hebrew title, by *Eretz Yisroel*, the Land
of Israel, the ancient and traditional Jewish name.
Jews have never called the country Palestine, which was
indeed a Roman name etymologically akin to Philistia.
Individual officers might sympathize with this insistence,

---

[1] "If the British Government appears to show a tendency to
wander from the straight path which leads to the establishment
of the National Home, or if it seems to be loitering along this
path, the Zionist Organization brings into action its extensive
resources of propaganda." *Survey of British Commonwealth
Affairs*, 1918–36, p. 459.

but the Government was undoubtedly right in resisting
a nomenclature intolerable to the vast majority of
Palestinians, and in substituting the device, relatively
inoffensive to all parties (though giving complete satisfaction to none), of adding to "Palestine" in Hebrew
the two Hebrew initials (E.Y.).

We cannot look ahead more than a certain distance; as
the Emperor William I answered Benedetti at Ems, no
man can guarantee anything *à tout jamais*. It may be
that the Arabs, spurred by honourable rivalry, will
attain a privileged position and a degree of civilization
inconceivable without Zionism.[1] The National Home
is beyond question unshakably established. Already its
numbers exceed that of the Cypriot nation.[2] If (as many
hold for their only belief), religion is dying, or if, with
the same result, some passionless Nordic creed should
reduce Holy Places to mere Ancient Monuments, then
Palestine would be an easier place to govern. Three
great faiths and a dozen denominations would look back
with incredulous pride to the battles each fought to
maintain its ideal. That time, if ever it come, is many
generations distant. But even if Mecca went, and Medina,
Jerusalem will bear it out unto the crack of doom;
and reasonable tolerance in the visiting and use of the
Holy Places—the Dome, the Sepulchre and the Wall—

[1] "Hospitable to various ethnic types and cultures, Palestine
has always been a Land of tribes and sects, and very seldom, if
ever, the country of one nation and one religion and under one
king." Sir G. Adam Smith, *Legacy of Israel*, p. 3.

[2] "There exists in Palestine to-day, as the result of fifty years
of Zionist enterprise, a Jewish National Home containing some
three hundred and fifty thousand souls, which fulfils the purpose
of a spiritual centre for Jewry. It is now possible for a Jew to
be born in Palestine and pass through an all-Jewish kindergarten,
school and University without ever speaking anything but Hebrew;
to work on a Jewish farm or in a Jewish factory, to live in an
all-Jewish city of 150,000 inhabitants, to read a Hebrew daily
newspaper, to visit a Hebrew theatre and to go for a holiday
cruise on a steamer flying the Jewish flag. So far the Zionist aim
may be said to be accomplished." Nevill Barbour, *A Plan for
lasting Peace in Palestine* (Jerusalem, 1936), p. 15.

will proceed not from agnostic indifference, but from sympathetic understanding no longer qualified by the fear that concession will merely invite encroachment.

Zionism is admittedly a departure from ordinary colonizing processes; an act of faith. To this extent, therefore, "impartiality" is condemned by Zionists as anti-Zionistic: he that is not for me is against me— a Mr. Facing-both-ways, like a Neutral in the War. Their attitude may be justified as anyhow constructive: you cannot make omelettes without breaking eggs: "to do a great right, do a little wrong." Will anyone assert that Palestinian Arabs can hope to have the predominance they expected, and but for Zionism would have enjoyed, in Palestine?[1] What is less justifiable (and much less helpful to the cause) is the assumption that the smallest criticism of any Zionist *method* or proposal is equivalent to anti-Zionism, even to anti-Semitism.[2] Such critics must remember that there are many good friends of Zion, there are even many Jews, who hold that the Balfour Declaration cannot be implemented by Great Britain or any other Mandatory because its parts are mutually destructive and incompatible, and that an unwillingness to recognize this can only breed gratuitous and unnecessary additional trouble: in short that unless we are prepared in the final event to see the history of the first coming repeated (when the fate of each group of inhabitants was that "they drave them utterly out") we should not have

[1] The Mufti is on unshakable ground when he declares, to the Royal Commission: "We have not the least power, nothing to do with the administration of the country, and we are completely unrepresented."

[2] " . . . There is no harm in that [divergences of Zionist opinion]; it only becomes dangerous when these different sections insist not merely that the object shall be carried out, but that it should be carried out precisely in the fashion that commends itself to them. Beware of that danger; I am not sure it is not the greatest danger which may beset you in the future." (From speech by Balfour to Albert Hall Jewish meeting in July 1920.)

supported Zionism. I cannot agree. The fact remains that we have supported Zionism; and we must continue to support it with undeterred but unhustled moderation and justice.

Nothing great has ever been easy, nor accomplished without deep searchings of spirit. Though I encountered —perhaps not less than others—some of the asperities of Zion, I could never understand the dullness of soul in Europe which failed to perceive that Zionism, for all its inherent difficulties and gratuitous errors, is one of the most remarkable and original conceptions in history. Concluding a public speech in London during the spring of 1921, after my first but before my second scouring in the Laver of Ablution provided by the Jewish World Press, I proclaimed the faith which after fifteen years, not excluding 1929 and 1936, I see no reason to recant:

"I have mentioned some of the drawbacks of living in Palestine, but you are not to infer that we are not fully aware of the privilege and honour we enjoy in serving there. In Jerusalem there meet, and have met for centuries, the highest interests of the three great religions of the world. From Jerusalem has gone forth at sundry times and in divers tones a God-gifted organ-voice, which has thrilled and dominated mankind. I do not dare to prophesy, for the East is a university in which the scholar never takes his degree; but I do dare to believe that what has happened before may happen again, and that if we can succeed in fulfilling, with justice, the task that has been imposed upon us by the will of the nations, and if we can reconcile or unite at the source the chiefs and the followers of those three mighty religions, there may sound once more for the healing of the nations a voice out of Zion. If that should ever be, not the least of England's achievements will have been her part therein."

. . . *Even now, in this thy day* . . .

The above section of *Orientations* was begun well before
the disturbances of 1936 and finished before the Royal
Commission had started for Palestine; with an occasional
footnote added in 1937. I have made bold to leave it
untouched; believing that its facts, inferences and
suggestions, so far as they go, are still perhaps less remote
from actuality than general opinion since the issue of the
Report would be disposed to allow. The main difference
of atmosphere with regard to the practicability of the
Mandate, between 1931—when I was last in Palestine—
and 1937 seems due less to the disturbances (which
could admittedly have been quelled much earlier),
or to the appointment, sojourn or historical analysis
of the Commission, than to their drastic and startling
recommendations. These, though as little expected by
the Government[1] as by the public, were accepted by
both with a surprising but not unintelligible alacrity.
True that, as in Parliamentary Debates during twenty
years of Incidents and Inquiries, the "unreasonableness"
of both sides (created by British and League Policy),
the "apathy" of the Palestine authorities (largely due
to lack of Home direction), and the admirable diagnosis
of the Commission each received an ample acknowledg-
ment from all Parties. The Palestine twins are shown to
be temperamentally irreconcilable, and the local practi-
tioners incompetent; the general applause being reserved
for the brilliant, if ultimately irresponsible, Consulting
Specialists. Nevertheless, to a stranger present throughout the Debates in 1936 there was in 1937 one startling

[1] As stated by Mr. Ormsby Gore in the House of Commons.

121

change of tone: the proved difficulties of preventing a
recurrence of outrage and humiliation had at last
established the existence of an Arab cause. There was
sparring for position between the Parties (curiously
reminiscent of the Spanish non-Intervention Committee),
as to how, and by whom, the Project accepted with such
resolution by the Government should be sponsored before
the League: all three reserving for themselves the
maxim: *La recherche de la paternité est interdite.*

There are Jews, Arabs, and British, who have worked
in Palestine more years than the Commission has months,
not only in official relations with "maximist" witnesses
keyed up, primed, and prompted during a period of
dreadful tension, but in daily personal contact with
Palestinians in their own languages, who are asking themselves—is the Mandate, accepting the first conclusions of
the Commission, so utterly unworkable ? How far do the
premises justify these second-thought recommendations?
Would not the sum-total of guards and of safeguards, of
cash and good will required to control three States, have
sufficed to maintain the Palestine Mandate ?

The Jews taste the bitterness of progressive disenchantment: the dream of the original Judenstadt; the
National Home, lopped, by the cutting away of Transjordan, to a Wales, and now pared down to a Norfolk.
And, even so minished, Zionism without Zion; "next
year in Jerusalem !" A heavy tribute of gold to a people
whose wealth they have already multiplied by ten. Into
whatever remnant of *Eretz Yisroel* can be spared from
Barracks, Customs, Coastguard, Passport and Quar-
antine offices, an ironic—a cynical *carte blanche* for
the immigration of world-Jewry. Irresistible overcrowd-
ing into necessarily concentrated industrialism: slums.
And the Arab answers: "Norfolk may be cramped
quarters for persecuted millions, but it represents a
large proportion of my East Anglia. Even assuming
that I must cut my losses in order to liquidate the Jewish

peril, then at least let it be with less vital sacrifices of my most fertile land, of my entire practicable seaboard. But why should I lose anything?"

There might, there should still be, no need. Once secured against the just dread of submergence by a Jewish majority; his grievances now recognized by the Mandatory and proclaimed to the League and the world, the Palestinian Arab might see fit to reason with his assumed adversary. The natural intelligence of the younger—and perhaps one or two of the older—generation might grasp the possibilities of close association with the greatest Empire, assisted by a power that preceded many and may survive most of the powers of this world. Jewish leaders may realize that, by declining to concede such an assurance or to content themselves as a slower increasing autonomous Palestine Community, they may indeed secure their majority, but it will be the majority of a pocket borough.

Meanwhile the lover of the Holy Land for its own sake, torn between intellectual assent and instinctive revolt, can only be certain that before any "solution" is super-imposed, far more serious efforts should be made to effect a freely negotiated settlement. Though both sides are for the moment confused by the strong wine offered of sovereign independence, compared with which all other draughts seem but an insipid dilution, they must by now surely have learnt their lesson—the insanity of shock tactics, whether by immigration or retaliation. Some have even concluded that the frightfulness of partition was contrived for the specific purpose of terrifying both into reason. But so long as the Arabs, by insisting on entire stoppage of immigration, and the Jews, by postulating an ultimate majority, refuse to take the first step towards agreement, there can be no hope of an accommodation that could be endorsed by America or approved by the League; and partition, hideous and hateful to all, stares them in the face.

P.P.S. 15. iii. 40

But facts outstared partition. The Woodhead Technical Commission appointed in March 1938 to advise on the practical effect to be given to these Recommendations of the Royal Commission found them to be, in effect, wholly impracticable, and by November 1938 had reported accordingly. As Lord Samuel wrote two years later "No solution can be hoped for by a geographical division of the country. The Peel Commission tried to do so. But the 'Jewish State' which it envisaged would have contained 46 Arabs to every 54 Jews; and one-third of the Jewish population of Palestine would have been left outside it"[1]. The British Government, in a too long deferred endeavour to achieve settlement by agreement, then convened the interested parties, Arabs and Jews, for a round table conference with the Colonial Office; warning them that, failing such agreement, they would "take their own decision. . . and announce the policy which they proposed to pursue". The delegates arrived in London. A fine round mahogany table was provided. There were conferences, for the Jews conferred with the Government and so did the Arabs. But since the Arabs declined to confer with the Jews there was no round table conference. In May 1939 therefore the British Government duly declared their policy, in a statement covering the three major aspects of the Palestine problem: Constitution, Immigration and Land.

In this document, the present charter of Palestine, they first maintain the promise of a national home for the Jews in Palestine, and lay down the process whereby they propose incorporating this home within an independent Palestinian State. Secondly, they regulate immigration at a total of 75,000 for the next five years, after which "no further Jewish immigration will be permitted

[1] Including representatives of the neighbouring Arab States of Egypt, Iraq, Saūdi-Arabia, the Yemen and Transjordan.

unless the Arabs of Palestine are prepared to acquiesce in it," and they undertake "to check illegal immigration".

Thirdly, since "the reports of several expert commissions have indicated that, owing to the natural growth of the Arab population and the steady sale in recent years of Arab land to Jews, there is now in certain areas no room for further transfers of Arab land, whilst in some other areas such transfers of land must be restricted if Arab cultivators are to maintain their existing standard of life and a considerable landless Arab population is not soon to be created, the High Commissioner will be given general powers to prohib it and regulate transfers of land ".

The first of these, the Constitution, can hardly assume form for at least five, perhaps ten years. The second, immigration, proceeded forthwith.

After ten months' delay, during which Arab observers began to wonder when—and even whether—the third item of Arab reassurance was to be fulfilled, effect was announced by the Palestine Land Transfers Regulations which, with a covering letter to the League of Nations were issued as a White Paper (Cmd 6180) on February 28, 1940. They were immediately assailed with a tempest of denunciation all over the Zionist world, mainly on two grounds: as tending to nullify the mandate and as disregarding the League of Nations. Neither contention can survive examination of the facts.

Arab land-fears are not imaginary. They have been confirmed by commission after commission of impartial and unprejudiced experts who have reiterated with increasing gravity the same warning—the danger of multiplying by steady, continuous erosion that most miserable (and dangerous) class, the dispossessed and landless peasant. Their cumulative demonstrations have been challenged but never refuted, and could no longer be disregarded.

Sympathy for Jews in the freezing hell of Central Europe will be extended to Zionists now confronted by the concrete application of what was till now but an abstract decision. Nevertheless, "these restrictions will not prevent the further development of the Jewish national home. Land purchases will not be stopped. They can be continued without restriction on a considerable scale in many areas".

Moreover, where so much has been accomplished in unique circumstances and under unexampled difficulties, it is as disingenuous as unfair alike to Zionist enterprise and British tutelage to minimise results and to concentrate upon such tendentious and provocative expressions as "ghettos" and "minority status."

To talk of ghettos in the face of the throbbing metropolis of Tel Aviv and of the shining Jewish colonies is an insult to both, just as the harping upon minority status must be interpreted by Palestinian Arabs as a thinly veiled menace. A population which under the mandate has multiplied ten-fold, from 50,000 to half a million, in little over a score of years, the free untrammelled development of Hebrew culture and institutions fully entitled Dr. Weizmann to proclaim in New York on January 16th, "What we have in Palestine to-day is a living organism whose growth no force can stifle."

The official Zionist argument that, "wherever the Jews have settled on the land the neighbouring Arab villages have benefited and prospered", though not without foundation, leads, if logically applied without check, to the conclusion that if only the Palestinian Arabs could become universal neighbours rather than owners they would live happily ever after—only where ? Not in Palestine. And when we are seriously informed that for "the plain man" these land laws "amount to the discrimination against the Jews on the grounds of race and religion which is forbidden by the mandate," we cannot but feel that he would have to be plain indeed not to perceive that a "discrimination" equally operative against non-Palestinian Arab or British Christian can hardly be termed an anti-Semitic measure or more "discriminatory" than the immigration laws of every Government in the world.

As for the insinuated flouting of the League, it will be remembered that, owing to the war, the Council was unable to assemble for discussion of the Mandates Commission report. In view, therefore, of the urgency of this already deferred legislation the responsible mandatory Government, in full possession of all relevant facts and considerations (many unknown to the general public) decided to accept the recommendation of their High Commissioner—an experienced Near Eastern administrator—and to act, and explain and invite League comment rather than to postpone indefinitely the third undertaking in its declared policy.

This policy was and is, like all "solutions" for Palestine, a compromise, wholly acceptable neither to Arabs nor to Jews. But as those who read the Press and have Jewish and Arab friends in Palestine are aware, it did result in a steady improvement of the situation. Meanwhile, the war broke out; Jews and Arabs, jolted back into reality by the superior horror of Nazism, *hostis humani generis*, began gradually to settle down to the experiment which both had in principle rejected; so much so that by February a mixed Arab-Jew contingent had arrived in France.

Nevertheless the Arabs had felt that of the three main stipulations of the policy, only the second, that of continuing Zionist immigration (to which they chiefly objected) had been put into effect. Between April 1st, 1939, and the New Year, 8,600 legal immigrants landed in Palestine besides 12,000 illegal (who were therefore deducted from the yearly quota). A little later 2,200 more illegal arrived, including (from no fault of the unfortunate refugees) several Gestapo agents. The actual fulfilment of what Arabs consider their third of the policy deepens their confidence. "A beam in darkness, let it grow."

Immediately the 1936 symptoms recorded on page 98 began to recur. One great daily announced in strict accordance with precedent, that "telegrams are pouring into the House urging M.P.s to resist the Government policy". They might well be. "Ministers and Opposition leaders are receiving a steady stream of telegrams from the United States protesting against the White Paper." No doubt. They were not the only protests we were likely to receive in a Presidential-election year.

There was a full-dress debate in the Commons, characterized by a general moderation and sense of actuality unique on this theme. The Secretary of State for the Colonies, Mr. Malcolm Macdonald, fairly routed his numerous opponents of all three parties, whose vote of censure was rejected by a Government majority of 163. It was time. We could not afford another 1936 in 1940. The allegiance of our Near-Eastern Allies and the good relationship of friendly neutrals had already been tested by events in Palestine and had hitherto not been found wanting. The rulers of Egypt, Saudi Arabia, and Iraq were no less embarrassed by the complaints of their Palestinian co-religionists than were our loyal Moslem fellow-subjects of India. This was no moment to strain them further. To reintroduce mistrust by even appearing to wobble upon this decision would have been to disconcert and unsettle the growing confidence of Palestinian moderates; to play gratuitously into the hands of the ex-Mufti of Jerusalem and his satellites, in cricket parlance to offer Dr. Goebbels a half volley, to which he would open his shoulders and which he could hardly have failed to lift over the pavilion.

Zionists were from their point of view doubtless justified in registering their protest, for in Palestine unprotested decisions are apt to be registered as accepted and the case to have gone by default. But the responsible mandatory Government is not only justified but, is bound in duty and in prudence to hold fast, and to see that both halves of the mandate are faithfully and practicably maintained.